SEEKING SHAMA

SEEKING SHAMA

Me, My Dog, and the Road to Inner Peace

KEE KEE BUCKLEY

Wellness Writers Press

WELLNESS WRITERS PRESS
An imprint of Pure Ink Press

Paperback ISBN: 979-8-9912047-3-6
Epub ISBN: 979-8-9912047-4-3

Library of Congress Control Number: 2025915878

Lyrics from "One of Those Years" written by Rick Kurek.
Used with permission.

Map illustration by Khayyam Akhtar
Author photo by Margaret and John Bohnel
Cover photo by Dawn Sinko

wellnesswriterspress.com
www.pureinkpress.com

In loving memory of Yoda;
I will carry you in my heart, always

For Mom and Dad—
who taught me that the journey is more than enough

For Eric—
who shows me every day what the meaning of love is

CONTENTS

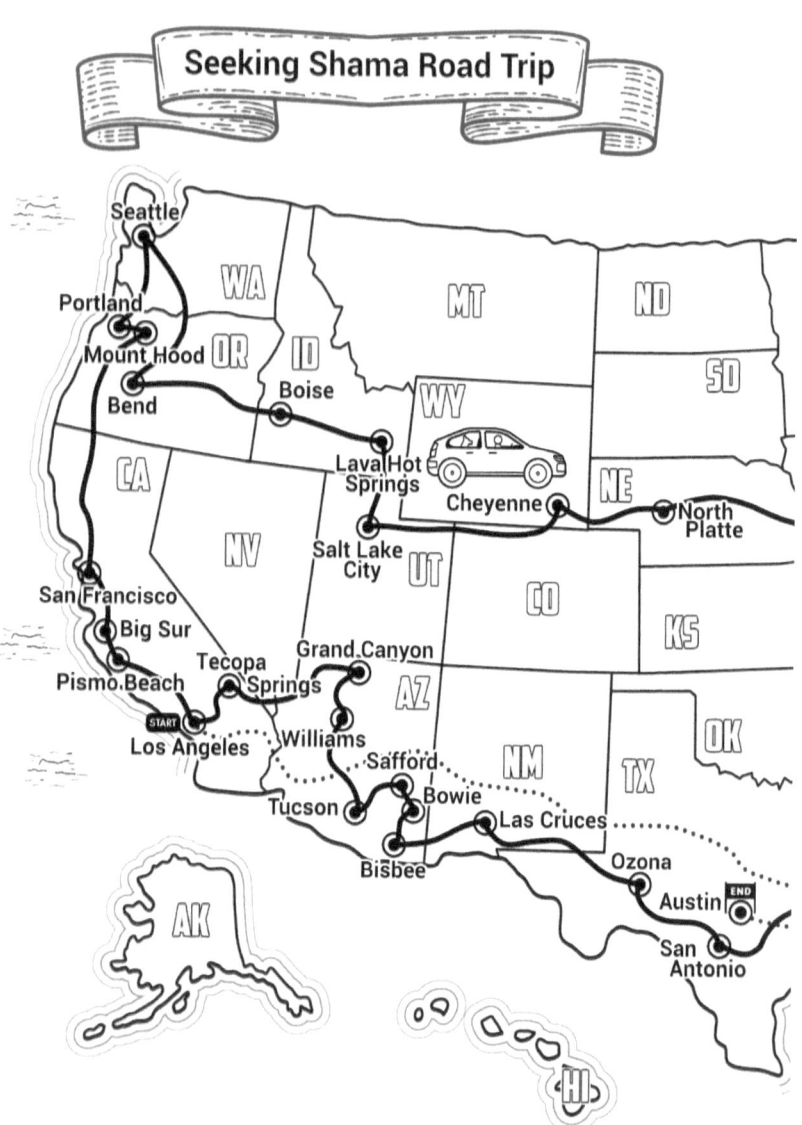

Seeking Shama Road Trip

AUTHOR'S NOTE

Writing this book over the past fourteen years has helped me reflect on and process the many wise lessons of the road. In crafting a cohesive story, I drew from my blog posts, journal entries, emails, photographs, social media posts, conversations with people featured in the book, and, of course, my imperfect memory.

I've done my best to stay true to the spirit of the moments and the conversations I remember. Five months on the road is a long time, and while I couldn't include everything, I've kept the events I chose to share in the order they happened.

To preserve the anonymity of certain individuals, I've changed names and identifying details.

INTRODUCTION
Los Angeles

The blueprint was foolproof, one that I designed and spent years meticulously constructing. My Los Angeles life was a house of cards balanced on the edge of an ocean cliff. Yet, the framework of a house of cards is, by its very definition, unstable. Each scene of life is represented by one playing card carefully propped against another—two stories, three stories, four stories high. But without a sound foundation, the slightest whisper of a breeze will cause the entire masterpiece to collapse, crashing down the steep rock face and splintering into a thousand pieces.

Work should never be more than a job; I realize that now. But back then, I built my career with a singular vision, long hours, and plenty of grit, and in the process, Hollywood became my identity. "What I Do"—make movies, lunch with important people, attend red carpet movie premieres, negotiate million-dollar deals—became "Who I Am." Working in a glamorous industry was intoxicating and had become all-consuming. As my number one priority, it outranked getting married or having a family of my own. With that much ambition and perseverance, I expected my livelihood to last until I was ready to retire. Instead—poof—in an instant, it was over.

I should have seen the cracks in the foundation. When one card fell, the entire structure of my life collapsed around me, driving home the point that my days as a type A overachiever were over. A swift and numbing rush of adrenaline paralyzed me. I was the architect of this fallen house of cards. I was forty-one and lived in a tiny five-hundred-square-foot apartment with an exorbitant rent. The love of my life had just resurfaced—the one who married and started a family with Rebound Girl—further rubbing salt in the wounds of my spectacular life failures: no job, no income, no boyfriend, no children, no safety net.

I still had my dog. *Thank God* I had my dog.

At that point, the admirable thing to do would've been to flex my spindly biceps, put boots on the ground, and rebuild. But instead, in the time-honored tradition of people wanting to run away from their crumbling lives, I got in my car, Princess Leia the Prius, with my dog, Yoda, and drove away.

I never liked road trips. Covered in crumbs from binge eating trail mix. Burnt coffee in gas stations. Sticky floors in truck stop bathrooms. Traffic detours that take you twelve miles out of your way. The saccharine stench of decomposing banana peels in the back seat.

But that was before 2009 happened.

The stagnant economy had turned into a global meltdown. People were losing their jobs, homes, and life savings; businesses were collapsing; retirement accounts were vaporizing; banks were failing; and the stock market was plummeting. The tanking economy had caught up with the film industry that had employed me for over thirteen years as a senior vice president of a major production company. I watched my friends in the business get laid off and then flail in the diminishing pool of available jobs. Now, I was joining them in the biggest blindsiding of my life.

It was a mixed blessing. Through the years, I began questioning whether making movies, a dream since childhood, should be my definition of success. It was quite a different mental space than the one I was in when I first started working in Hollywood, where the production company I worked for was on the Paramount Pictures lot. Every morning after parking my car, I would gaze at the Hollywood sign nestled in the hills in front of me. These giant white letters that I had seen in so many movies were now staring back at me as if to say "You have arrived!" In those early days, I had to remind myself to breathe. I was doing more than walking onto the Paramount Lot—I was walking into my dream of working in the movie business.

The Paramount Pictures lot is a magical place. Paramount is the last major film studio remaining in the Los Angeles neighborhood of Hollywood, which lends it an air of old Hollywood glamour. It's filled with history-laden buildings that house offices and soundstages, and rumors persist of hauntings by movie stars of bygone eras.

On my first day of work, while walking to my office, a golf cart zipped past, whisking Dustin Hoffman in the opposite direction. An actor from *Star Trek* rode past on a bicycle, wearing a prosthetic creature head and everyday clothes. He was on his way to wardrobe. It took all my willpower not to stare. Right before I entered my office building, a dog trainer walked by with a Jack Russell terrier strutting alongside him—Eddie, the dog from the TV show *Frasier*, which was filmed on the soundstage directly across from my office. How did a Wisconsin girl like me end up in the middle of Hollywood? The feeling that I was on the precipice of finding greatness swept me away—greatness in all those around me, not necessarily in myself.

Soon, my life filled up with power lunches, A-list parties, and movie premieres. But everything I ever thought would make me happy, didn't. Despite its glamorous façade and obvious perks, working in Hollywood became mechanical and empty. All glitter on the exterior and no substance at the core; not all things shiny and sparkly on the outside are diamonds.

It was complicated, though. I couldn't afford to leave my job. Fear about paying back my student loans for law school followed me. My degree wasn't a well-thought-out plan—with my natural-born instinct to avoid conflict at all costs and instead withdraw into myself, being a lawyer was never in my blood. Riddled with student loan debt, which sucked, I needed the paycheck to meet my exorbitant monthly student loan nut. I was stuck, fearing what would happen if I left a good job and that my peers would reject me if I lived outside the status quo.

Even though I was unfulfilled, my apprehension about walking away from my paycheck and a career I had once dreamed about kept me firmly tethered. So, when the layoff came, I was shocked to be kicked out of the club.

Welcome to The Great Recession.

A road trip probably wasn't the most brilliant plan, given that I hadn't created an itinerary and I have rules regarding driving: I don't drive at night, in the snow, or with less than a half tank of gas. And absolutely, under no circumstances are bananas allowed in the car. I did, however, have a shining beacon of hope guiding the way in the form of a faded decade-old sticky note plastered to the dashboard that read, "I Welcome Change."

We'd drive until I found *shama*—a Sanskrit word that means peace, tranquility, and quietude of mind: things people usually find on a yoga mat, not on a busy highway.

PROLOGUE

Pacific Coast Highway

One, one thousand; two, one thousand; three, one thousand. Counting the swishes and squeaks of the windshield wipers is reassuring, as if I'm bringing order to the chaotic unknown. I'm trying not to worry, but worrying is what I do best. *Four, one thousand; five, one thousand; six, one thousand.*

Early October rain pummels the car's hood as we drive, sounding like popcorn erupting inside my grandmother's cast-iron Dutch oven. A Hummer passes in the opposite direction, and the tap dance of water spraying the windshield temporarily drowns out the whooshing of wind over the curves of the car topper. The ocean is barely visible through the coastal fog and sheets of rain. With me in the car is the only thing from LA I can't live without: my dog, Yoda.

Eddie Vedder's "Society" is playing from my road trip playlist. Part of the soundtrack to the movie *Into the Wild*, the song is about society's materialism and, ultimately, about leaving it all behind because it's never too late to change one's life.

The palm trees sway dramatically in the cascading rain, and the gloomy road matches the thick cloud in my heart and the tears on my cheeks. With a deep inhale, I resolutely look onward to the traffic in front of me. Positive change lies somewhere up ahead.

The call of the "road less traveled" is loud, with the possibility that time alone might clear away the messy detritus of Hollywood from my brain and allow new dreams to germinate and bloom.

Yoda snuggles deeper into his pillowy bed nestled in the back hatch of the car. He's ready—so long as we are together, provided he has a window with a view. Am I ready? There is no guarantee I will find my way or even *like* the girl left standing at the end of the day. With no promise that the road will lead me to where I am meant to be, it's not as though you can set your GPS to shama: "Hey, Siri, give me directions to inner peace."

Certainly, this unconventional dark night of the soul or vision quest is tossing my restrictive life playbook out the window; I'm following the magnetic pull to drive and seek out shama. My place in this world. My true north. My peace.

Taking a cue from Eddie Vedder, it's never too late to change my life.

ONE

Pismo Beach

Yoda is standing on his bed in the back of the car, hackles raised and breath fogging a small patch of the window already smeared with his doggie nose art. He's making a sort of excited warble as he looks out the window. A Yoda yodel.

"What is it, Yoda?"

He whines loudly and quickly looks back and forth between me and some horses grazing in a field next to the highway in Malibu.

I laugh. I can always count on Yoda to lighten the mood.

I've filled the last few days with making lists, shopping, trial packing, and leaning on my dad for help mapping out a loose itinerary for this first leg of my trip. Although I've never been a fan of road trips, my dad loves them. He and my mom take at least one road trip each year, so it's quite fitting that he was the one to help plan my possible pit stops for the first week on the road. I called him up last week after returning from the Santa Monica AAA office where I had picked up the same maps my dad had gotten from his local AAA office.

"In my hand are all the maps for the Western States. I really can't believe we're using paper maps, Dad."

"Your GPS will only show you about fifty miles ahead, but we can plan long and alternate routes by spreading out our maps," he said enthusiastically. "I like to see the big picture and the minutiae that a paper map provides. If you're looking at your GPS screen, you lose the details of the little towns."

"I guess you're right, and a paper map will never randomly route me through a lake because of construction."

"In my book, that would be a good day on the road, so long as I have my fishing pole with me," he said, laughing. "Take your time and explore the road. We'll be waiting for you to arrive by Thanksgiving."

Warmed by my dad's love and support of my adventure as I cruise through the countryside, I consider my goal of landing in Wisconsin by Thanksgiving to spend it with him and Mom and my sisters and their husbands and kids. I have no idea how long it will take me to get there. It could be one week, or it could be a month. It feels important to stay flexible and let the road dictate where I go and what I learn.

"Maybe getting out of the fast lane and embracing the existence of potholes, roadblocks, and detours will lead us along life's scenic route. Right, Yoda?"

He lets out a whimper coupled with a yawn when the field of horses is no longer in view, then spins in circles a couple of times and settles back into his bed.

Yoda's been in my life for almost six years. I adopted him on November 11, 2004. I remember it vividly—the morning I was finally going to get a dog. I had wanted one for years but made excuses like: I work too many hours to own a dog; the yard isn't spacious enough; if I get one dog, then I'll probably end up wanting a second to keep the first one company and my small apartment is not big enough for two—yada yada. Yet, in one short hour, all of those excuses went out the window when I learned that my boyfriend of three months was cheating on me. Instead of crying and replaying our conversation over and over while trying to figure out what I could have done differently, the only thought in my mind was *It's time to get a dog.*

A few weeks later, I was standing on the sidewalk at Boxer Rescue LA, overwhelmed by meeting dog after dog that the patient volunteer brought out of the kennel; they all needed homes. I had thought it would be an easy process and that I'd immediately feel a connection with a dog. That wasn't happening. There was no explosion of oxytocin, the bonding hormone, or something else that might cause me to look at a dog with absolute certainty that we would become family.

"I have one more dog to show you," declared the volunteer. "We've had him for three weeks, and you're the first to meet him. He's about eighteen months old and is a mixed breed of boxer and French bulldog, so we're worried we'll have trouble finding a home for him because he isn't purebred. We've named him Brownie."

Brownie had a cowlick on the top of his head—a tiny mohawk—and a glossy, reddish-brown coat with patches of white on his paws, belly, and tip of his tail. With his eyes locked on mine, slowly, the tail tucked between his legs started to curl up over his back. Still, his bouncy ears stuck out like bat wings, and his forehead crinkled in worry or anticipation; I wasn't entirely sure which. I crouched down to meet Brownie and gazed into his large caramel-colored eyes. He trembled as he moved forward, burrowing his forehead into my chest as I wrapped my arms around his silky-smooth coat.

"We see this all the time," the volunteer said, beaming. "Humans don't adopt the dogs. Dogs adopt the humans."

Tears were streaming down my cheeks. Where did those come from? Oh, oh, oh! I was getting it. This precious creature was The One. He was my dog.

"Do you want to go home with me?"

In response, he pushed his crinkly forehead harder into my chest, almost as if he couldn't get close enough.

I decided his name would be "Yodhaka," or "Yoda" for short, a Sanskrit word that means "little warrior," which really fit him because he had been living on the streets.

Two hours later, Yoda jumped out of the car and ran around my small Santa Monica yard, lifting his leg to mark every inch— laying claim to his new home. As soon as I opened the door, Yoda ran inside. After he smelled everything, I showed him his bed. We sat on it together, me with my legs crossed and Yoda lying with his head on my lap. He sighed and closed his eyes in exhaustion.

I gazed down at him, stroking his baby-soft fur, and tenderly explained that I had waited a very long time for him. "I promise to always love and protect you," I whispered, "and your forever home is now with me."

Yoda sighed again.

My chest was tight; my heart had swelled to ten times its normal size out of love for this little creature. We were family.

The next morning, before I headed to yoga, I put Yoda in a crate I borrowed from a neighbor. He was panting and trembling when I latched the door, but I stuck my fingers in, stroked his face, and told him I'd be home soon.

With each sun salutation, I dedicated my practice to my new dog. Slowly wandering home after class, complete contentment engulfed me now that I'd joined the ranks of dog owners.

My serenity screeched into a shocked halt as I opened the door and almost slipped in a huge puddle of Yoda's saliva. He was jumping on me, yelping, and panting with excitement, or relief, that I was home. *Oh crap, why isn't Yoda in his crate?* Across the room, I could see he had bent the wires on his crate from breaking out of it. *Damn, what is he, Krypto the Superdog?* I checked his mouth and was surprised he hadn't broken a tooth. Deep gouges marred the front door, and he had gnawed a chunk out of the molding around the entrance—this damage would be expensive to fix. *Okay, so Yoda doesn't like to be crated.*

The next day, when I left him alone again, this time out of the crate, I hurried through Whole Foods, throwing dinner ingredients into my cart and rushing through the checkout line. I was only gone an hour but returned to find Yoda sitting on my front doorstep with my neighbor, who had discovered him just as he was about to jump through a screened window that he had ripped out. Splintered wood chips were on the floor, and he had punched a hole in the door, which showed me it wasn't solid wood.

This less-than-seamless entry into each other's lives was not what I had mapped out in my head. My new dog wasn't supposed to complicate my life; he was supposed to make it better. Yoda slunk over to me and licked my hand. He looked so sad, guilty, and distressed with his furrowed brow.

"It's okay, sweetness." I muscled through a cloud of concern. "I won't abandon you. We'll figure this out together." I wasn't sure how we'd fix it, but I was determined. After pouring a glass of wine, I opened my computer and hit up Google.

My research about separation anxiety proved that I had my work cut out for me if I was ever going to be able to leave him alone—it could take months of desensitization training. Some cases of separation anxiety are so severe that dogs can never be successfully left alone. *My dog may never improve.*

To cap it off, I have a natural tendency to worry, which makes things worse. I have always had a secret anxiety about things not under my control; the disquiet settles faintly below the surface. The unease is there, and although it doesn't have a viselike grip over my life, it still softly chatters away in my ear. I've worried about everything from how dismal I feel at work, to my parents driving on icy roads if a snowstorm is walloping Wisconsin, to not living out my plan for my life. Yoda didn't understand my worrying nature; he only wanted to protect his human and always be together—my shadow and me. If I was anxious about leaving him alone out of fear that he'd hurt himself or escape and run away, then he'd pick up on my energy and panic about being separated from me. A vicious cycle. A catch-22.

The ultimate irony about me having adopted Yoda is that I worried all the time about not finding a partner and forever being alone in life—Yoda and I both worried about being alone, yet here we were in this together.

Now, six years later, Yoda and I are a solid team. He still has separation anxiety, but with the help of doggie daycare and the generosity of dog-loving dog-sitting friends, we've made life together work.

Yoda is perched comfortably in the back. His ears perk up and he does a double take when we make eye contact in the rearview mirror. Ask any *Star Wars* fan, and you'll learn that Yoda is the wisest being in the Universe. He is. I swear. Yoda rescues me every day since he first saved me from my broken heart when I adopted him. He gets me out of bed on the mornings when I want to pull the covers over my head and hide from the weight of the world. He burrows his forehead into my chest when I'm sad, as if he's desperately trying to get as close as possible to comfort me. He presses his back against mine in bed—a nice reminder that I'm not alone.

Pulling into a Pacific Coast Highway gas station, we do our dance: Fill the tank, stretch, take Yoda for a quick walk around the parking lot and nearby grass, tell him to jump back in the car, fasten his seatbelt, and kiss him on the top of his head.

Yoda looks up and cocks his head, making his little bat ears stick straight out. I look into his eyes and find what I've long believed: the soul of the Universe can be seen in the eyes of a dog.

He looks so much like that other Yoda of *Star Wars* fame, the most powerful and masterful of all Jedi Masters. I have a sneaking suspicion that he's in my life for a reason—to teach me something. Maybe he'll be guiding me on this journey—Canine Soul GPS. Much like the Jedi—representing good fighting the evil Sith—perhaps my Yoda, who is currently staring at me with those piercing wise eyes of his, is here to help me learn to master the Force (sans lightsabers) and use it to create healthy change in my life. Without him, I'm not sure I could do this trip alone. It's taken some balls I don't have. So, I borrowed his. Gotta give him props for that.

The car door clicks shut, and I walk around to the driver's side. Thick, humid ocean air mists my face as I look across the Pacific Coast Highway. Untamed waves wash over the rocks and sand before they retreat, and the water is sucked back out to sea. The movement of the waves is unpredictable, yet fluid. Is that also how the road is going to be? Here we are, the three of us—Yoda, Princess Leia the Prius, and me—heading into the unknown. With the Force and Yoda at my side, we'll drive to, oh, I don't know, wherever we're supposed to be. Timbuktu, Oshkosh, Shipshewana, Dagobah.

When I climb back into the car, a sticky note stuck to my dashboard catches my attention, and my eyes sting when I read the words I scribbled ten years ago. During eleventh-hour packing and organizing last night, I randomly reached deep into the back of my junk drawer and was astonished to pull out the old sticky note—a little buried treasure from the past.

Years ago, doodling tornadoes while negotiating a high-profile actor deal on the phone with a smug talent agent convinced that the world revolved exclusively around his client, I realized I didn't care about this actor. I didn't care about the movie he would star in. While the agent rambled on—"Blah blah blah, my client needs three massages a week, blah blah blah, his personal trainer needs to be on the set, blah blah blah…"—I wrote "I Welcome Change" on a yellow sticky note pad on my desk. That night, I stuck the note to the gearshift in my car so that I would see it every day during my long, traffic-congested commute to and from my Hollywood office.

For the next few months, I constantly doodled "I Welcome Change" on sticky notes at my desk. My screensaver was "IWC," and I whispered "I Welcome Change" after each frustration at work or at home.

My sticky note mantra had me analyzing my complicated relationship with Harry, my live-in boyfriend/partner/six-year-love-of-my-life. Behind a curtain of perceived sexy jobs, palpable passion, and passports filled with traveling the world together, we grappled with what seemed like two insurmountable issues: my insecurity and Harry's commitment phobia. Never believing I was good enough for a man as worldly-wise as Harry, I spent our many years together trying to prove to us both that I was, simultaneously morphing myself into a woman I thought was indeed worthy of his love and tackling the mystery of unmasking my identity as a young adult. Meanwhile, Harry worked hard in therapy to conquer his commitment phobia: "It's not about my love for you. It's about my harrowing fear of abandonment."

Harry was born in England, where he was raised with world travel, museums, and classic literature. He held passports for three countries. I was born and reared in Wisconsin, preferred long hikes in nature to art exhibits, and was more apt to read adventure-driven dystopian fiction than Tolstoy. Yet, despite our differences, we flourished as a couple. We were as comfortable reading the Sunday paper together in bed in our Venice Beach house as we were waking up to geckos climbing the walls of a beach bungalow in Thailand. We met on a blind date soon after I moved to Los Angeles in 1996, and Harry's calm, reassuring presence helped me navigate both a new city and a new job in Hollywood.

Yet Harry's reluctance to put a ring on my finger led me to obsessively wonder whether he questioned if there was someone better for him.

And so it was that I made one of the hardest decisions of my life—in the spirit of my then-one-year-old sticky note mantra, I made a change. Almost six years after I met the man of my dreams, I left him.

Last night, after unearthing the "I Welcome Change" sticky note from the drawer, tears filled my eyes as I turned it over in my hands. The note is weathered, faded, and torn, yet its message still carries weight. Even though the job is long gone, I'm no closer to real change than when I first scribbled those words.

After performing a makeshift laminating job with packing tape, I adhered the sticky note to Princess's dashboard with duct tape, so now it is center stage on this road trip. A beacon of hope and guiding inspiration.

Five hours after leaving LA, we land at our first overnight stop. Given the recent state of my emotional health, it makes sense that the first sleep of the trip should be in Happy Town, USA—a week ago, *Parade* magazine reported that San Luis Obispo, on California's central coast, is the happiest place in the country. Gimme a shot of that Kool-Aid, please. It's crazy, but with God as my witness, the rain briefly stops, and the sky slightly clears just as we drive into the area. Cue the angelic music.

After parking Princess at a dog-friendly, run-down Pismo Beach motel, I leash Yoda and we head toward the ocean to stretch our legs. The beach is empty, given the dreary, wet weather. The sun, peeking through a break in the overcast sky, shines a pinkish hue on the craggy rock formations and little caves at the back of the beach. It's peaceful and still, even with a fine mist falling from the sky. While Yoda sniffs and paws curiously at piles of wet seaweed on the sand at the end of his leash, I sit on a rock and watch the waves roll in. It seems fitting that the beginning of this trip consists of rain and muddy paws.

To some, I might sound ungrateful for the life I'm leaving behind—the glitz of working in the film industry, cuisine from some of the country's best restaurants, yoga classes alongside famous actors, daily walks on a windswept beach, and weekend hikes in the scenic coastal mountains to find remote waterfalls and panoramic views. Nonetheless, without having lived and breathed its essence daily, it's hard to understand how numbing LA can be to one's spirit. It is an intoxicating place, home to an industry that thrives on youth, physical beauty, fame, and wealth. Not a beautiful starlet in the first quarter of life, I'm an unemployed introvert—an invisible wallflower standing at the sidelines of life, too insecure to join the dance.

As a pod of dolphins slowly swims past, performing their synchronized act, I remember what an ex-boyfriend's sister once told me. She's a shaman, called to the path from a young age, with a deep connection to the aquatic world. She said dolphins have a message for me, and that I need to pay attention whenever they show up.

As a spirit animal, the dolphin is a reminder to breathe new life into oneself consciously. Whereas the autonomic nervous system controls human breathing—we don't need to think about taking a breath because it happens automatically—for dolphins, breathing is always a conscious act. That's why only half of their brain shuts down when they sleep; they need the other half to stay awake so that they can breathe and not drown. Dolphins hold their breath for up to ten minutes, and once they decide to inhale, they first exhale fully through their blowhole before filling their formidable lungs with oxygen.

A cool thing about being human is that even though breathing is usually an involuntary function, we can still consciously control it, and by doing so, we can better manage our emotions and energy levels. When I have anxiety—like now—my breath is shallow and rapid. So, embracing the wisdom of the dolphins, I inhale slowly and deeply, hold it for a count of ten, and then gradually exhale fully to discharge heavy energy and negative mindsets intentionally. It works—I feel lighter.

Many stories about dolphins describe how they save people or guide off-course boats to shore, deeming the dolphin a protective totem to bring guidance and assistance into your life when you feel lost. *Hey there, dolphins, I'm over here. Help me find shama.*

Yoda looks up with sand on his nose and cocks his head as if to say "Lighten up, Ma."

Dolphins also symbolize the importance of playfulness in keeping us from getting lost in the seriousness of life. *Oh boy, is this reminder ever timely.*

Yoda executes a wet dog shake to dry off, then looks up with his tail wagging. It's time to get moving.

Standing up and brushing the wet sand off my jeans, I grab Yoda's leash, and we walk up the beach toward music playing in the distance. It turns out to be the 64th Annual Pismo Beach Clam Festival right beside the beach. People are milling about the artist tents while others stand under umbrellas in the drizzle, watching a band play on the covered stage. Being a dog-friendly event, Yoda feels at home and sips water from a public dog bowl. The blissful aroma of cumin, oregano, and garlic drifts through the air, and my stomach growls. Having not eaten a real meal yet today, I'm ravenous. After purchasing a steaming bowl of spicy clams and rice from one of the vendors, I sit on a curb under a tent to eat. Yoda sits next to me, drooling, staring at my bowl. I toss him a dog treat from my pocket. "This is mine, Yoda, and that is yours."

I'm wearing my late grandpa's worn, frayed, and paint-stained green army shirt as a jacket, and my dad's "Hogs are Beautiful" 1971 belt buckle to carry them with me on the road so I'm not all alone.

Six young men dressed in military fatigues wander over to say hello to Yoda.

One of them sits on the curb beside me and introduces himself as Scotty. "Pretty cool shirt there. It looks like it has history."

"Thanks. My grandpa wore it in World War II. I wear it when I want to feel close to him."

"That's dope."

"What are you all doing here at the Clam Festival?" I ask.

"We've just completed military training and came here to grab some food. Next week, we're shipping off to our next destinations."

"That's exciting, congratulations. Are you nervous?"

"I grew up in a small town in Tennessee and figured joining the army is a great way to experience the world," he proclaims. "I'm a little scared but also really excited."

Our journeys are so different, but at the same time, just like Scotty, I'm both—a little scared and really excited for what comes next.

The following morning, after filling my coffee travel mug in the lobby of our motel, I approach the woman behind the front desk and see she's eating a jelly donut, with sugar on her fingers and a bead of red jam at the corner of her mouth.

"Good morning. I'm just passing through Pismo Beach and wonder if there's anything I shouldn't miss here before I leave."

She wipes her hands on her pants. "Oh yes, there is! The Pismo Beach Monarch Grove is only a half mile down the road."

"Oh, that sounds lovely. What can you tell me about it?"

She swallows another bite of the donut and hands me a tourist brochure. "We have the largest gathering of monarch butterflies in the country. Every winter, thousands migrate here and cluster in the limbs of a grove of eucalyptus trees. It's cool to see."

Oh yeah, I can get into this.

Butterflies symbolize rebirth into a new life. That is me—totally me. This road trip is about seeking change to find shama and transform, so what more perfect a way to kick off a self-discovery road trip than by being surrounded by thousands of butterflies in the limbs of towering eucalyptus trees? A message from the Universe. *Show me the way.*

When Yoda and I arrive, I stand in place with my eyes closed, relishing the minty-pine, slightly menthol fragrance in the air. People seem to either love or loathe the medicinal perfume of the eucalyptus tree's waxy blue leaves. I'm in the prior category.

We walk for an hour through the grove, futilely searching for any sign of a single butterfly. Nature isn't cooperating. It seems we've arrived too early in the season. *Thanks, Universe.*

Crestfallen, as we turn to leave, I see a small cluster of monarchs on a branch high above us. The monarchs have only just begun their voyage to Pismo Beach, as I have only just begun my journey. Huh. The symbolism is freaking perfect, after all.

Metamorphosis cannot happen overnight. It's not exactly the lesson I expected from the road, but it's a good one. Yoda has a spring in his step, which I'm pretty sure means he agrees.

TWO

Big Sur

After loading up Princess with Yoda and my duffle bag, we continue our sloshy drive up the California Central Coast toward Big Sur for a night of camping. In the spirit of embracing outer silence to find inner peace, I seek the stillness and solitude that nature so readily provides.

Even in the rain, this part of the country has a beauty that I will never tire of. The dramatic undeveloped coastline is one of the most scenic driving routes in the country, and the water grows bluer and clearer the further north we travel. Reflecting on the symbolism of the Pismo Beach monarchs, my journey's rainy, weathered beginning is like that of a lotus flower. Eastern philosophy views the lotus as a symbol of rebirth and spiritual reawakening. After growing in muddy, murky waters, the lotus emerges in pristine white or pink hues, symbolizing the rising from life's hardships. So, out of my muddy life, there will come...? Something beautiful.

I pull off Highway 1 just north of San Simeon to see the elephant seal colony at Piedras Blancas, protected by a nonprofit organization called Friends of the Elephant Seal (FES). Even though October is still early in the season, at least a thousand of these giant silvery-coated sea mammals are beached on the sand, looking perfectly content, napping in clusters in the chilly downpour. I open my umbrella as I step out of Princess, leaving Yoda in the car, and I walk toward the seals.

Up to 17,000 elephant seals will gather on the beach in a couple of months. These enormous creatures have their name because the large nose of adult males resembles an elephant's trunk. According to FES's website, fully-grown males can grow up to sixteen feet long and weigh up to 5,000 pounds. Even the pups are huge, weighing around seventy pounds. The elephant seals move by hurling their bodies forward and then flopping down onto their bellies. Several of the males lift their chests, point their faces to the sky, and, with a bit of bravado, make a loud vocalization that sounds like a drumming lion roar. They seem to be vocalizing when other seals are flopping their bodies along the beach, coming closer. They must be warning them not to get too close. Or maybe it's a mating call? They aren't moving fast enough to know for sure.

One hundred years ago, the species was presumed extinct from hunting. But, after a small colony was discovered on Guadalupe Island off the west coast of Mexico's Baja California Peninsula in the 1920s, legislation and marine mammal conservation efforts allowed for the elephant seals to reclaim breeding territory safely and rapidly grow their numbers. In 1990, they commenced their annual journey to Piedras Blancas to molt, breed, and give birth.

I planned this visit with these captivating creatures, unlike my first encounter with elephant seals.

Soon after we started dating in 1996, Harry took me on my first California road trip, and we ended up on this exact beach. After a tour of the nearby Hearst Castle, we parked the car on the side of the highway to walk on the sandy beach. Harry reached over and clasped my hand, our fingers intertwining. The mesmeric pull of our passion-driven new love meant we were always touching in one way or another. With wide eyes, we stepped into a pod of elephant seals sunning themselves on the sand. Walking amongst the magnificent giant mammals, we took photos and marveled at this gift of nature bestowed on us. It was a crisp autumn day, and I was wearing Harry's sweater and feeling very much in love. That was then.

This is now, and I am standing by myself in the rain on a wooden tourist platform, observing from behind a protective fence built a couple of years after we discovered this magical beach. When I continue walking, the downpour completely soaks my jeans, and now the wind keeps trying to turn my umbrella inside out. I'm shivering—and pensive.

Four days ago, I saw Harry for the first time since we broke up nine years ago.

Although we email once or twice a year, he made it clear to me years ago that he didn't want to see me. After getting engaged to his pregnant then-girlfriend (now wife), he sent me a message telling me that although we'd stay in touch via occasional emails, we couldn't ever see each other again because it would mess him up too much. Really? Okay. He was going to make this new relationship work. It stung—I had secretly held out hope over the years that we would get back together one day. But at the same time, I respected him for establishing boundaries. Since then, I've kept cool and detached in our infrequent email exchanges. I've moved on too, falling in and out of love with other men, leaving Harry in the past, convincing myself that I'd found closure.

But then this week, he emailed out of the blue to tell me that when he and his family were moving to their new house, he found a box of my belongings in the attic of the Venice Beach house that we had lived in together. He wanted to give it to me. So, we agreed by email to meet for happy hour at a popular outdoor lounge of a Santa Monica hotel.

The instant I saw him sitting on a poolside sofa, looking my way, I felt the sizzle of the palpable current between us, flowing as strong as ever.

"Hi," he said in his buttery baritone, ever-so-slight English accent, rising to his feet as I approached.

"Hi," I echoed.

What else was there to say, standing before my first love with a pounding heart and throbbing loins, catching my breath, and carrying the knowledge that he found happily ever after without me despite all that?

We hugged briefly and awkwardly, although, for a millisecond, the feeling tempted me to hold on too long and melt into those arms I hadn't had around me in what felt like a lifetime. After ordering drinks, we stiffly sat on the sofa facing one another. My hand sprung to my neck and twirled my necklace, an involuntary action that happens when I'm nervous. Harry has always had an electrifying presence, one that exudes confidence while at the same time inviting me in closer. He also has a sense of humor that, when we were together, made me laugh at unexpected moments.

"Awkward," he sang dramatically as he swirled his glass of wine and looked to the sky. It broke the tension and I laughed.

We made small talk about his booming business and my lack of work.

"We've gone global and now have satellite offices in Dubai and Tokyo."

"Oh my gosh, that's fantastic. And to think that I knew you when," I teased.

His production company was small and only a couple of years old when we first started dating. After graduating from film school, he and his partner launched it out of their apartments.

Fluent in Japanese, Harry directed and produced commercials and documentaries for many large Asian companies.

"So, you've left the movie-making world, huh?"

"Not by choice," I humbly muttered. "My career has pretty much dramatically imploded."

I studied his face while filling him in about getting laid off. He hadn't changed much. I noticed a few new wrinkles around the eyes when he smiled and some strands of silver at his temples mixed in with his dark, wavy hair. For the most part, though, he didn't seem to have aged. His short sleeves revealed the birthmark on his arm. How did I forget that? I used to love tracing my fingers around it—a move right out of a Hallmark movie. Whatever. I think it's obvious that this flick never moved past the second act.

I wrapped the review of my current events, saying, "I'm kinda lost about what is next for me. I'm going to take a long road trip. Maybe I'll never come back. Is that crazy talk?"

Harry gazed at me thoughtfully.

Right after I said, "I think LA might be done with me. Or maybe I'm done with LA. I'm not entirely sure," he glanced at the time on his phone and, looking pained, almost as if I had said something that deeply wounded him, abruptly announced he had to leave.

We left our virtually untouched glasses of wine and walked to our cars together, him mumbling something about having to relieve the babysitter.

Before turning away to cross the street toward his car, he said, "I forgot your box."

I didn't believe him. Especially when he followed it up with, "Let's have lunch in a couple of days before you leave. I'll bring the box then."

Two days ago, we met for lunch at Gypsy Café in Westwood. I was a few minutes late due to traffic after dropping off Yoda at doggie daycare. Harry was already seated at an outdoor table when I arrived.

"The restaurant name may not be politically correct, but it seems suitable since you're about to embark on a life of wanderlust with your dog."

I laughed. Harry laughed. Our eyes met, and then we both quickly looked away.

The meal progressed, we relaxed, and the conversation became more real. When Harry showed me photos of his daughter on his phone, there shone in his eyes a light that I had never seen—pure, unconditional love—and I felt happy for him after all our years of struggling with his fear of commitment. *How wonderful that, finally, Harry knows how to love.*

He scrolled down to a close-up photo and handed me the phone. "She looks so much like you," he said. Then, with a grin, "How did you pull that one off?"

Was this what our daughter really would have looked like? She was beautiful, like a little glowing angel with pink cheeks, big blue eyes, and curly blond hair. When Harry and I met, it seemed written in the stars that we would have children together. He was supposed to talk about our children and me with that same light in his eyes. How did that not happen? Why did I leave this man? How did he let me go?

Harry reached over the table and lightly touched my arm. "I always thought you would be a natural mother."

Lifting my chin, I forced myself to be calm and breathe while trying to remove the dagger from my heart discreetly.

"I'm sorry, Kee Kee. I feel as though I took that away from you. I made a mistake. I just wasn't ready when we were together."

Not knowing how to respond, I busied myself with attempting, unsuccessfully, to split the bill with him.

After lunch, he suggested that we walk to Diddy Riese, a nearby ice-cream shop that we always went to for ice-cream sandwiches made with freshly baked cookies. They used to be only fifty cents per sandwich, but now the prices are up to $1.50.

"Let me guess, you want chocolate chip cookies and vanilla ice cream," predicted Harry.

"My hair may have changed, but my sweet tooth hasn't," I bantered, hoping I sounded witty. "I bet you want oatmeal cookies with salted caramel."

"Ha, yes. We are both creatures of habit."

We started walking the three blocks back to our cars to hand off my box.

"Marriage suits you. You seem really content."

After a pause, his shoulders slumped, and a weariness swept over his downcast eyes. "Things aren't very good at home. She just asked for a divorce."

I was afraid to breathe.

"We never should have gotten married. But I don't want to break up the family, so I don't want the divorce—"

I held my breath.

"—even though we don't love each other."

His words ending that sentence plunged the dagger deeper to finish the job of slicing my heart in two. At that point, I needed a shot of whiskey, not ice cream. I wanted to yell, "But I'll love you! She doesn't love you and wants a divorce, but I'll love you! Forever. I always have and always will. I promise!" Instead, I turned away, tossed the remnants of my melting ice-cream sandwich in a sidewalk trash can, and heard my voice crack as I spoke. "I'm so sorry to hear that. I hope you'll be able to work it out."

When we got to our cars, Harry carried the box to my trunk and placed it inside. Our eyes locked. Then, he reached out, pulled me in, and hugged me tightly, this time not letting go. As I surrendered to our embrace, his arms felt simultaneously so familiar and so foreign. When we finally pulled apart, tears pooled in his eyes.

"Now you know why I told you I could never see you again. My feelings for you are still so overwhelming, even after all these years."

I'm not sure how I remained composed as I responded. "Somehow, our lives took us in different directions, Harry. But you will forever be to me the one who got away."

Standing here all alone with the elephant seals, I raise my face to the sky, squeeze my eyes shut, and give up on the umbrella, letting the biting wind and rain whip my skin, as if in an act of self-flagellation. Ten years ago, I welcomed change when I created my "I Welcome Change" sticky note mantra. Did I make the wrong change when I left Harry? Maybe I should have found a new job, not a new man.

Should I have fought harder for us? Would things be different if I had? Or does the foolish, out-of-control, hopeless romantic in me wish for another chance with Harry? Will I ever get a satisfactory answer? Probably. Definitely not. Maybe?

When I return to the car, I open the door, and Yoda gives a happy whine. After climbing in, I shift around unsuccessfully to adjust my waterlogged jeans so they aren't sticking to my thighs. Oh, Harry.

During the first few years after we broke up, periodically, we took turns sending an email about missing the other person when one of us found ourselves single. However, the timing was always off, with the other one dating someone else when this reaching out would happen. My life didn't stop when we broke up. I found love again several times, but I'd be remiss if I didn't admit that perhaps, on some subliminal level, I compared all the men in my life to Harry. Earth to brain—stop, just stop.

I look at Yoda in the rearview mirror. He's grooming his paws.

"Yoda, what if I had fought for him? Did I ever truly open my heart to the idea of him coming back into my life?"

Yoda briefly looks up and then goes right back to licking.

Did I purposely keep the door closed to Harry out of fear that he would reject me if I invited him back in? Was not knowing if he would ever commit better than knowing that he never would? Good ol' self-doubt—just around the corner when you need it.

The fact of the matter is, you don't know. Is this thing alive, or is it dead? Do I sprint forward or run back? Should I have done something different? Do we belong together? All the nights awake, wondering. All the brain hours trying to figure it out. More often than not, you'll never get the answer, and you must live with that and keep on moving on.

After several hours of driving, Yoda and I arrive at the Fernwood campground in Big Sur. Our home for the night is a tent cabin under the ancient Coastal Redwoods on the bank of the Big Sur River. Besides two other tents and a couple of RVs on the far side of the campground, we have the place to ourselves, possibly due to a mix of the inclement weather and it being a Sunday night. When we pull up to our spot, wild turkeys and deer are grazing near our tent—nature, front and center.

A few hours of daylight remain, so after changing out of my wet jeans, I take the camp manager's advice to visit a couple of nearby scenic spots before settling in for the night. We first head to Partington Cove to see its kelp forest and playful sea otters. Kelp forests are a fascinating and vital underwater ecosystem. Kelp is used in everything from toothpaste to ice cream and has even been talked about as a potential renewable energy source. I pick up a piece that has washed up on the shore. It's as big as a fire hose, and the texture is rubbery instead of slimy, as one would expect. The surf makes the kelp forest sway in unison like a flowing underwater ballet, and my manic mind chattering begins to slow. Nature is starting to work its magic.

Leaving Partington Cove, we have time before dark to drive to Pfeiffer Beach. It's hard to locate with the turnoff hidden and involves driving for two miles down a pothole-ridden, one-lane unmarked road. However, with detailed instructions from the camp manager, I find it. We park and hike a short distance to one of the most beautiful, secluded beaches I've ever seen—and we have it all to ourselves. Instantly, the exquisite salty beach air hits my nose and arouses all my senses. The sand has a lavender hue, rock carve-outs jut into the water, ocean cliffs tower over us, and the crashing waves spray water ten feet skyward. It doesn't matter that it's still raining—the clouds open enough for the sunset to project golden light over part of the beach.

With my drenched hair matting my face and Yoda giving his sopping-wet fur a shake, I feel a sense of freedom. Standing here, waterlogged, with my dog, in the face of this awesome scene is just what I need. I've escaped from LA, and although I have no idea how long I'll be on the road, I know I won't be going back there for quite some time. While feeling that way about a place that has been my home for almost fifteen years is daunting, the potential for change is exhilarating.

Suddenly, Yoda's feeling the freedom, too. His muscles quiver, and his ears perk up, sending the universal dog message that he needs to run. So off go the sandals. I roll up the cuffs of my jeans, and together, we sprint up the beach on the wet sand. I'm smiling for the first time in months—actually laughing out loud—as I try to keep up with him.

We reach the end of the beach, and Yoda leaps over a rock and pivots to face me. He crouches down with his butt in the air in a doggie play pose with his tail wagging wildly. I face him and crouch down, too. We both mock-charge each other, trying to psyche the other out. Yoda's ears lift with happy mischievousness. Suddenly, he charges toward me, dodging sharply at the last minute to run around me.

Stopping to catch my breath, I sit on a moss-cushioned log with a tide pool at my feet. Yoda, panting hard, pads over and flops down next to me. We are looking through a large arched rock formation in the water, balanced in front of the setting sun—a seeming portal to a secret magical land, like the wardrobe in *The Chronicles of Narnia*. A symphony of pink and fiery red colors shimmers across the water, bathing me in optimism—a shot of caffeine to that long-slumbering mindset.

It's dusk when we arrive back at the camp, and with a break in the rain, I build a campfire. After I get into dry clothes and rub Yoda down with a towel, I clip his harness to a thirty-foot tie-out cable that I connect to a picnic table so that he has freedom to roam without me having to hold his leash. I fill his bowl with kibble, and we eat dinner by the light of my headlamp. The simplicity of my meal makes me savor every bite: two hard-boiled eggs, an avocado purchased from a roadside stand, kettle corn that I impulsively bought yesterday when leaving the Clam Festival, and a single-serving bottle of wine. It's chilly, so I'm wearing two fleece jackets, a knitted hat, and a scarf around my neck.

I love camping and have even experienced rugged camping in the middle of the Amazon rainforest. Fernwood is hardly hardcore camping. Although there's no electricity and I had to bring a sleeping bag I borrowed from a friend, the campground has bathrooms with electric lights, there is a convenience store up the hill, and I am in a canvas tent cabin (meaning it has a wooden floor and a door with a lock). Still, as I sit in the dark with my dog, next to the dying embers of my campfire, I realize this camping experience is by far my most ambitious. Why? Because I'm doing it by myself. I'm not scared in the dark. I built my own campfire. I'm going to snuggle in my sleeping bag alone tonight. Although my fingers and toes are numb from the cold, there is no place in the world I would rather be at this moment. The crisp chill in the air makes me feel alive, almost as if an early winter wind feeds the feeling I had at Pfeiffer Beach and helps it grow.

My favorite moments with Yoda involve burying my face into the soft fur around his neck. That's my happy place. So, after this day of exploration and freedom, it's what we are doing now—snuggling together in a campground, far from the bright lights of LA.

"I'm happy we're here together," I whisper.

I'm committed to moving forward and staying open to what happens organically on this road trip, and because of that, I'm beginning to see the first hints of my inner lotus flower emerging from the muck.

What a lesson of the road this one is.

Om shanti shanti shanti. Bring forth the cosmic peace.

Right, Yoda?

He's asleep.

THREE
San Francisco

Yoda and I get up early after our night of camping in Big Sur. We didn't sleep well at all. Even burrowing into a down sleeping bag while wearing my outerwear, with Yoda snuggled next to me covered in a wool blanket, I shivered all night.

He didn't know what to make of sleeping in a tent, so Yoda did what dogs often do when perplexed: he kept asking to go for a walk, which he did six times during the night. He'd stand up next to me and stare. He'd shake himself if I didn't move, making his dog tags jingle. There would be no choice but to climb out of my sleeping bag, grab my flashlight, and walk him. Each time, he'd lift his leg to fake pee and shoot blanks, then look up at me with guilty puppy eyes as if to say, "Honest ma, I thought I had to go."

By the time the sun rises, I am anxious to get moving. We pile into Princess, and I crank the heat as we continue driving up the coast. We're headed to San Francisco to see a few friends who live there. Onward!

Something about being a transplant in a big city makes a select few of one's friendships deep and meaningful. Since we don't have relatives living near us, our friends become our local surrogate families. We spend holidays together, and they collect our mail when we're out of town, are our emergency contacts, watch our pets, know our house alarm codes, and have spare keys to our front doors. I am blessed with a handful of these friends in Los Angeles.

As I was tossing and turning last night, I thought about not taking the time to say goodbye to my LA "family" before leaving town. I was in such a sorry emotional state that I didn't want to check in with anyone. All I wanted was to don the invisibility cloak and disappear. I have failed so miserably in my own eyes that I didn't want anyone to see me this way. I don't have a family of my own, and I don't even have a boyfriend. So, without my career identity, even though I didn't like that career, who am I? I couldn't face my friends because I couldn't face myself. So, I just left.

To make up for my guilt about my departure, spending time with my friends in San Francisco seems extra important—as if that'll make it okay.

After a few hours of driving, including a couple of pit stops to walk on dog-friendly beaches, we enter the San Francisco metropolitan area, which expands the two-lane highway into eight lanes and bumper-to-bumper traffic. Every muscle in my body tenses up. In three short days, it's become clear that driving through the country relaxes me, and city traffic stresses me out. Imagine the stress hormones that have been pumping through my body during my many years of daily commuting in LA on some of the most congested freeways in the country. I have a lot of detox to do, and San Francisco traffic is not helping.

We arrive at my high school friend Aaron's house in Oakland around 5 p.m., dirty and tired after our night of camping. My friend Jake, who recently moved to San Francisco from LA, pulls up at the same time as Yoda and me. After hugging Aaron and Jake, I make a beeline for a much-needed post-camping shower. Aaron performs his culinary magic in the kitchen, and Jake gives Yoda some much-appreciated fun by playing tug of war with his toy.

When we sit down for the first course, heavenly pumpkin pear soup with fresh sage, I present Aaron with a bottle of wine as a thank you for his hospitality.

"This bottle of V. Sattui Angelica is a mix of Muscat and nineteen-year-old pot-still Carneros brandy. I hope it's every bit as posh as it sounds."

Indeed, it tastes like a fine bourbon, and the three of us savor every sip from our cordial glasses. It is so rich that one small glass is enough, meaning most of the bottle remains.

"Do you plan to see many friends on your trip?" asks Jake.

"Well, I don't have much of a plan after this first week," I muse, "so I honestly don't know. I hope that friends of friends will hook me up with the occasional sofa or guest room so I can minimize the credit card charges for hotel rooms. Basically, I'm wingin' it."

Aaron clears his throat. "I'm not going to accept your gift of wine."

"What? Why not?"

"Look," he explains, "the Angelica will keep for at least three weeks. So, take it with you and share it with all the old and new friends you meet on your trip."

After a moment's reflection, I think this is a damn good idea.

"Hmmm, a traveling bottle of delicious wine. One that I will get to enjoy each time we uncork it. Hell yeah!"

While Jake and Aaron continue talking, my mind wanders. *Will I meet any new friends on this trip? Or will I finish off the bottle in a hotel room alone in the middle of nowhere? Stop it, brain.*

When Aaron heads to work in the morning, Yoda and I spend the day wandering around Sausalito, a city at the northern end of the Golden Gate Bridge that has waterfront restaurants, art galleries, and boutiques. After scarfing down a cheese sandwich in the car, I find a charming pet-friendly waterside café where I order coffee and write in my journal. Sitting in these idyllic surroundings, I'm inspired to write that there may be life after LA. I spent years captivated by the place and its promises of a happy, exciting, and never-dull life. I was addicted to the *hope* of finding those things in LA, but never did. I was also locked into the path I chose for myself, not wanting to admit that the road I was on was a dead end. I'm probably similar to a recovering junkie at the moment, fighting to reconcile my need to find a fix for the unfulfilled promises of my old life, with the hope that I'll find a healthier life if I leave it all behind. It's a tangled mess. But, like pulling on the loose thread of a sweater, it's starting to unravel.

Late in the afternoon, Yoda and I head to San Francisco to spend the night on Jake's sofa in the Mission District. Once we arrive, an impromptu dinner party ensues, and the guests are all special friends of mine. Aaron joins us, as does an LA yoga buddy, Krista (who moved to the Bay area a couple of years ago), and Holly, a friend from back home in Wisconsin. It gives me so much joy to round up my friends and see them all laughing, talking, and getting to know one another while Yoda takes turns laying on each of their laps. He's in heaven—so so so much attention.

As the five of us toast with small cups of my newly christened traveling bottle of wine, I have a quiet moment of wonder as I look around the table. Here I am, an utter mess. I am jobless, broke, lost, and confused, yet these friends still love and accept me. What a revelation. I don't need the sexy Hollywood job, fancy title, or thick wallet to be accepted. These friends are here for me, supporting me on my crazy journey to find myself, opening their homes, and sharing their food. My friends love me just because I'm me. Maybe part of finding shama is that I need to accept myself, in all my goofy glory, without apology, just because I'm me. In this first week of my travels, this lesson of the road may be the best thing I've learned.

Now I must go out and live it. "Come on, Yoda, let's get on with it."

FOUR

Mount Hood

An important rule of travel is to be flexible with your plans. The same goes for life: be flexible. Things rarely go as intended, so the more open you are to change, the more likely your trip will be a success. Again, just like life. Through my travels, I've found this to be true time and time again, most recently when Delta Air Lines lost my luggage this past summer, leaving me to attend a girlfriend's wedding in Tuscany and then "backpack" through Italy *without* my backpack. I've always been pretty good at rolling with the punches when it comes to travel. But after a lifetime of careful, cautious planning, I've yet to master putting this rule into practice in everyday life.

When I arrived in Rome, my backpack didn't. Delta had no idea when it would show up; they couldn't even track it in their system. However, I didn't have time to get upset because I had a small window to board a train to Florence, luggage-free, to meet Jesse. We were both friends of the bride, but we had never met. Since we were both single women, the bride connected us, thinking that we might want to travel together.

When I got off the train, Jesse was standing beside the tracks waiting for me, and it was friends at first sight. She was wearing a chic white sundress and pink cat-eyed shades. With her long blonde hair and tall, lithe figure, her aura was more like that of a glamorous movie star than someone planning to lug her backpack around Italy with me.

Instead of taking in the art and history of the city, we spent the next twenty-four hours running around buying my essentials: shoes and a dress for the wedding that I snagged straight off a mannequin in a window, a couple of cheap sundresses, a swimsuit, and a small leather bag in which to carry everything. We rented a car and drove to Tuscany for the wedding, and then, because we were having so much fun together, we continued via train to Venice. I called Delta each morning, only to hear that they still didn't know where my backpack was. I resigned myself to the fact that I wouldn't see my belongings on that trip.

As I wore the same two sundresses day after day and borrowed toiletries and makeup, I relished the fact that *I had no stuff.* I didn't have to decide what to wear, and without hair products, my hair could only look one way: slung up in a ponytail. Without international service on my cell phone, I stopped obsessing about my dying career back home. By being present with my situation, the stress in my life melted away. Having no baggage was liberating. Losing it did wonders for my state of mind.

At a pre-wedding dinner for the backpack-less wedding, I hit it off with a friend of the bride, Ben. We were seated next to each other, and our conversation was light and flirtatious. The wedding took place in an olive grove, followed by a dinner, where we sat together outside at tables overlooking the cypress trees and the sun setting in glorious colors over the scenic countryside. Ben and I danced together and then even went for a midnight swim at the bed and breakfast where everyone was staying. A group of us, including Jesse, traveled the next day to Montecatini Terme to see its famous mineral springs and architecture. Then we all went stand-up paddleboarding in Lake Bilancino's clear, emerald-green water. All the while, Ben and I were never far apart. Italy has a passionate culture, and the picturesque rolling hills of Tuscany opened me to romance. When he left the following day to return to America for his work, we exchanged contact details, knowing it would be a long-distance relationship, given that he lives in Oregon and I'm in California.

In the following week, Jesse and I shared an array of adventures—including a double date in Venice with gondoliers on their gondolas (something I never knew was on my bucket list, but in retrospect, it should have been right at the top)—to which I wore the mannequin-sourced dress I'd purchased for the wedding. Before Jesse left Italy, we promised to keep in touch since she lives in Seattle.

I spent a few days solo in Rome before my flight back to LA, which was not necessarily a good thing. My backpack finally caught up with me, so I was no longer baggage-free—both literally and figuratively. As I wandered alone in that city of art, architecture, fountains, and love, I began to feel the burden of my life's baggage. The last time I'd been in Rome had been with Harry, and reminders were everywhere. I wandered past the Piazza Navona and stumbled upon the small hotel we'd stayed at thirteen years earlier. I indulged in decadent tartufo gelato from Tre Scalini, a legendary place that Harry and I had visited every day. I dined on the patio of a charming café that we'd discovered together. While walking to the Pantheon, I ended up in a small piazza where Harry had swept me into his arms, dipped me, and passionately kissed me in front of an ancient yellow building with cracked and flaking paint.

One night, I was sitting at the base of the Trevi Fountain, a baroque fountain built by the Ancient Romans with Travertine marble. It has witnessed centuries of transformation, from the rise and fall of the Roman Empire to its ultimate restoration and growth into modern-day society, and the Trevi Fountain has remained a symbol of the Eternal City.

But instead of being fully in the moment with one of the most famous fountains in the world, I wallowed in a spray of self-pity, locked in the thought that there I sat, heartbroken over losing Harry nine years earlier. Is it possible that love can be eternal, like the never-ending city of Rome? All I could think was that if I hadn't left Harry, I wouldn't be sitting there alone, and he'd be helping me sort through the mess of my life. I was annoyed with him for moving on, marrying someone else, and having a family without me. We should have attended my friend's wedding in Tuscany together and then vacationed in Italy as a family with *our* kids, throwing coins over our shoulders into the fountain to ensure our return to Rome like all the other tourists. My mind started to obsess about the possibility of Harry getting divorced and finding his way back to me. I know I shouldn't have, but yes, I went there. All the way there. But who can blame me? Freakin' Italy, it impacts the heart. After all, Venus, the goddess of love, was a Roman deity.

After I flew back to LA, my connection with Ben continued. We've been casually dating long-distance for a couple of months now. He visited me once in Los Angeles, and I visited him once at his beautiful house that overlooks the Columbia River Gorge outside of Portland. Since we live so far apart, our romance has developed slowly. Nonetheless, Ben is smart, well-traveled, athletic, and a nice distraction from Harry.

As luck would have it, Ben is currently in San Francisco on business. Since the timing works out perfectly, he is joining Yoda and me in the car instead of flying home.

However, as we drive the first of two eleven-hour days, it becomes clear that we are a terrible match. Our conversation is awkward, and we're both forcing polite small talk.

"So," I say, clearing my throat, "when should we stop for the night?"

I don't want to miss any of the magnificent Redwood National Forest that we're driving through, and I'm not comfortable driving at night, so I'm hoping to stop soon.

"I have to get back earlier than I thought and deal with work," he says, meaning we need to power through and drive at night to make the journey, with only one overnight stop instead of two. He just played the work card, so I sigh in defeat and keep driving.

Then, around 11 p.m., while driving through the pitch-black darkness of the forest, flashing red and blue police lights appear behind us.

"Oh my God, Ben. I'm being pulled over." I steer the car onto the shoulder of the highway and stop.

It turns out I have a burned-out taillight. The officer is nice, but he still issues me a fix-it ticket, meaning I must find a place to repair my taillight, have the ticket signed by a state patrol officer confirming I've resolved the problem, and then mail it to the courthouse to avoid a fine.

"Don't drive at night until you have this problem fixed," says the officer.

"We will go straight to a hotel and not drive until morning," I promise. "Can you tell us where we might find one?"

"The closest town with a motel is forty-five minutes ahead."

"Thanks, officer, for being so nice. I'll get the taillight fixed right away," I tell him with a tired but apologetic smile.

As we pull away, Ben and I don't speak at all. I'm fighting the urge to say something snarky about how this wouldn't have happened if we hadn't been driving at night, and I'm sure he's itching to scold me for having a burned-out taillight on my car. The air is thick with tension.

Almost an hour later, we arrive at a tiny town in Northern California, the name of which I don't even know, and the only room available in the run-down motel is a smoking room. While I take Yoda for a quick walk, Ben hauls in what we need for the night. Then, we both collapse into the lumpy queen bed. Ben immediately falls asleep, and I lie awake, noticing my nose feeling increasingly stuffy from the tobacco odor clinging to the sheets. The moonlight is casting creepy shadows off the popcorn ceiling. I don't want to be here with him. I don't want to share my car with him. Or a bed with him. I want this to be over. To be alone. With Yoda.

The next morning, Ben eats pancakes by himself at a diner that shares a parking lot with our motel, and since I can't leave Yoda alone, my furry shama warrior and I walk to a nearby market. Tears of frustration threaten to spill over as I sit on the curb juggling yogurt, a cup of coffee, and Yoda's leash. Like me, I am sure Ben is counting the hours until we are no longer cooped up in a car together. But for now, we must survive another eleven-hour day of driving in the rain—eleven hours of hell. Check, please.

In fairness to Ben, in my emotional state, I only want to share my road trip with Yoda. I want to be alone and do what I want to do *when* I want to do it—like having the freedom and privacy to cry when I listen to my road trip playlist—and I don't want to drive at night, dammit.

When I began my road trip, I expected to feel lonely and crave companionship. I thought Ben's protective embrace would comfort me and make me feel less lost and alone. However, as it turns out, the opposite is true—I'm exhausted from pretending to be positive and in high spirits since I first saw him yesterday. I'm unable to keep up the act any longer. So, when we finally arrive at Ben's house at 9 p.m., I waste no time putting off the inevitable.

We are standing in his living room, having just carried in our bags.

"I suppose we should talk about what's been on both our minds since yesterday," I say. "I think it's probably clear to both of us that there isn't a romantic connection between us after all."

He looks confused. Then frustrated. And finally, peeved.

"Why would you say that? Being trapped in a car would make anyone cranky. That doesn't mean there's no future for us."

It turns out that despite our lack of connection during two days of driving (without even one kiss), Ben has still been holding out hope that things will get better once we get out of the car.

What's becoming clear is that our disconnect during this trip is due to me. I've had a wall up, and without realizing it, I've been adding layers of emotional concrete to it the more time I spend with Ben. He has no chance of breaking down that wall, which means a relationship between us doesn't have a prayer.

I have been desperate for someone to save me from writhing around in the sticky web of life. Yet, in less than a week on the road, I've already learned that I need to spin a new silk thread to rescue myself. I need to do the work if I am ever to make changes in my life that will lead to inner peace. I am seeking shama, and it is clear I'm on a solo journey. There are no shortcuts. I must do the work alone to get there.

Ben isn't happy with me, but at least he lets me stay the night, since it is far too late to find a hotel room.

"Do you have extra bedding?" I ask. "I'll just tuck myself in on the sofa." It's going to be a long night. The sofa is a small black leather loveseat that is great to look at, but hardly conducive to sleeping.

"Don't be silly, Kee Kee. There's room in the bed for both of us." He genuinely feels bad for me and is trying to extend a small olive branch.

We spend an uncomfortable and awkward night sharing his bed, me hugging my side of the bed, and him hugging his.

The next morning, we sit in the kitchen drinking our coffee.

"I'm sorry you feel you have to leave," says Ben. "Are you sure you don't want to spend a couple of days here?"

"I have the itch to keep moving. I think I'll find a hotel in Portland, since I haven't spent much time in the city."

Ben gives me a sad but kind smile. "I need to leave for work, but you and Yoda are welcome to stay while you figure out your plans. Just lock the door behind you when you take off."

He hugs me before heading to his car, and then I get on the case to find a Portland hotel. Not knowing the city at all, I haven't a clue where to begin looking. So, I make an SOS phone call to my friend Beth Howard, aka the Pie Lady. Beth is an internationally loved writer who used to live in Portland before I met her years ago in Los Angeles, and now she lives in the American Gothic House in Eldon, Iowa. Yeah, that one. The house in the iconic Grant Wood painting.

Upon hearing a two-minute summary of my predicament with Ben, and just as I begin to say I'm worried about paying big-city prices for a hotel and perhaps should stay in a suburb, Beth interrupts and says, "Give me thirty minutes, and I'll find a place for you and Yoda to stay."

Half an hour later, I load up my car, and Yoda and I head to Mount Hood to stay with Beth's friend Martha. On the way there, I stop at a garage and have my taillight fixed. The mechanic tells me that it's a law that I have chains in my car this time of year, in the event I get caught in the snow. So, I buy a set, and after his quick demonstration, I tuck it away in my car topper. Let's hope I don't need chains, since I'm not confident I will remember how to put them on. Then I drive to the nearby State Highway Patrol office, where an officer signs my ticket to confirm I've corrected Princess's taillight problem. After I walk Yoda around the parking lot, we climb back into the car and continue to Martha's house.

While visiting the mountain wasn't on my itinerary, it's liberating to let go of my travel plans and see what the Universe presents. It's usually a gift. In this case, we drive through miles of fruit orchards straight toward the snow-capped mountain and arrive at a heavenly mountain home on twenty acres of forest, complete with a teepee, hot tub, full guest apartment, two friendly dogs, and a fire pit. So many gifts! However, the best surprise of all is Martha herself.

She meets me at the front door with a friendly smile and a mug of hot tea.

"Welcome! I made you a cup of mint tea to help you settle in. This rain can chill you to the bone."

It's amazing that this woman, who had never heard of me until this morning, is so welcoming. Martha is a creative, spirited, and fascinating person. I am most impressed by her fierce independence. She lives a rich country life in this wooded mountain home, doing everything from chopping wood to scaring off a bear threatening one of her dogs. While I was fending off drunken executives in Hollywood, she was fending off 600-pound mammals with inch-long claws that can run 35 mph. She wins.

Martha hands me the keys to the guest apartment and tosses Yoda a treat.

"Any friend of Beth's is a friend of mine. You're welcome to stay for as long as you like."

"Be careful what you offer. It's so cozy here that you may never get me to leave."

"Take time to enjoy the hiking trails. I groomed them myself," she says, giving Yoda a belly rub. "But keep an eye on Yoda. I had a house guest a few months ago who let her Lhasa Apso run free, and sadly, we never found him. I'm still broken up about it."

The guest apartment is comfortable and warm, with a living room and kitchenette. There's a picturesque view of Mount Hood through the sliding glass doors of its private entrance. It is *still* raining, which makes the apartment feel extra cozy. It would be divine to curl up with a book under Martha's down comforter, but Yoda is wagging his tail while alternating looks between the door and me—code for wanting a walk. Instead of being frustrated with the almost constant rain during this trip, I'll embrace the cold drizzle. Bundling up with a scarf, gloves, and hooded rain jacket, I'm ready to venture outside.

"Let's go, Yoda. Time to explore."

Yoda is a city dog with a high prey drive. If a squirrel or cat is nearby, he'll fixate and either won't hear me calling his name or will purposefully ignore me. Leash walks are a given because I can't trust him to stop and look both ways before crossing a street.

At first glance, Martha's forest seems the perfect place to let Yoda run free. Unfortunately, we have more than squirrels or cats to worry about here in the woods. Bear scat is all over the property, and having heard about Martha's dog's recent brush with a bear and her warning about her previous guest's lost dog, I keep Yoda tightly tethered to me. He's wagging his tail in excitement, and his nose is working in overdrive as we hike one of Martha's trails. Yoda has lived his entire life in Southern California, so I can only imagine the sensory stimulation going on with him right now as he explores the scents of the Pacific Northwest. His intense focus indicates that his olfactory receptors have revealed a galaxy-spanning macrocosm.

The cool mountain air is so sparkly clean that I want to gulp mouthfuls of it to fill my lungs. Douglas fir trees envelop me in a soft blanket of their woodsy, pine-like scent. A big-leaf maple has just dropped a yellow leaf larger than my head, and a gentle breeze becomes its dance partner, swirling the leaf around before gracefully releasing it to the ground. I've found nirvana on Mount Hood. Yoda impatiently tugs on the leash to get me moving, shaking me out of my reverie.

My time on the mountain is a welcome reprieve from all my driving. While it's only been a week since I left LA, it seems much longer. During my stay here, Martha takes me under her wing. The first night, she invites me up to the main house for pizza and blueberry pie with her friends. Another night, she takes me to a dinner party. Twice during my stay, Martha and I break out the traveling bottle of wine, sipping from our glasses while we talk late into the night about the complicated journey of life. She left a fast-paced career as a marketing executive and later an exciting life with her Olympian ex-husband, exchanging it for a simpler life on the mountain. She is content and happy with who she is. Gimme some of that, pretty please.

One evening, I dig out my jewelry-making supplies that I stowed in a corner of Princess Leia's car topper. I brought them along to make thank-you gifts for people who give Yoda and me a place to sleep. As the rain patters on the roof, I wire wrap a necklace with several different gemstones that capture Martha's energy: blue obsidian, smoky quartz, and carnelian.

After three days, I wake up and something tells me it's time to move on. It's interesting that, without having a set schedule, I can sense my guidance system, and it's waving the green flag. I'm getting the urge to discover what's ahead, so it's with bittersweet emotions that I prepare to leave the mountain. I fill my water jugs with the freshest water I've ever tasted (straight from the glaciers and into the tap!), pack up Princess, and then say goodbye to my new friend, Martha. I give her the necklace that I made, and she sends me off with a bag of organic apples freshly picked from a neighbor's orchard and a jar of applesauce she made this morning.

Already in this first week of my road trip, I've experienced the disappointment of things not going according to plan, followed by the joy of realizing that something far more delicious can take its place. Letting go of plans and allowing life to unfold naturally is my most recent lesson of the road. Kind of like "go with the flow."

FIVE

Portland and Seattle

Beth has arranged for us to stay a couple of nights in Portland with her friends Ally and Brett, and our drive toward the city takes us through the lush Columbia River Gorge. The river cuts through the Cascade Mountains, bordered on one side by Oregon and on the other by Washington. Basalt cliffs hang 1,000 feet above the river like towers of a cathedral, and waterfalls and cascades of various sizes speckle our route.

Multnomah Falls, the Taj Mahal of Oregon waterfalls, is the perfect place to stop for a hike and stretch our legs. A thunderous 620-foot plunge of spring-fed water flowing over moss-covered rocks fills the misty air with a damp, earthy perfume. Always on the lookout for hidden symbolism, I consider what this waterfall represents. It could be the washing away of the stagnant parts of my life that aren't working, or it could mean I'm about to tumble off a cliff. Which is it? Possibly both. Am I using this road trip to run away from a broken life? Maybe. But even in these virgin days of this spiritual journey of trying to find shama on the road, I've already learned that you can run away from everything but yourself. I'm stuck with yours truly. So, even though I don't know how to fix my life, and despite leaving everything behind (friends, a non-existent career, an apartment for which I'm still paying rent, an ex-boyfriend I can't stop thinking about), maybe there's a method to this madness.

I send a silent prayer into the ether for answers. To whom, I'm not sure. To the God of my Christian childhood, to Buddha, to Krishna, to our collective consciousness, to my higher self, to the Divine, to a great force of untouchable and unknowable energy that makes up the Universe, to the source of all things— they all mean the same to me, and I sure hope they are listening.

It just *has* to be part of the Universe's master plan. Source knows what it's doing—life's hurdles and roadblocks occur so we can learn that a steady and unwavering inner peace exists underneath it all. That's the shama I seek. The winds may whip the waves of life into a frenzy, but deep beneath the surface, there are always still waters. Then again, if that's the case, and shama is always with me, why can't I dive down far enough to see it?

In this first week on the road, I've noticed the effervescence of some initial sparkles of healing. My tears are no longer constant, and I've sometimes found myself smiling. Progress! However, finding shama is a monumental feat that I'm not sure is possible. I have no idea how or if I'll find inner peace, but I do know that I can't go on living the way I have been.

Eyes open. Heart open. Let's go.

We pull up outside Ally and Brett's house and sit in the car for a moment, engulfed in the charm of the old Victorian homes in their neighborhood. The autumn trees bear brushstrokes of amber and crimson, and beams of sunlight break through gaps in the clouds, making the raindrops on the leaves twinkle like little fairies. Climbing out of the car, I take a deep breath and walk to the front door with Yoda at my side.

Ally and Brett have a magnetic, outdoorsy energy about them, and they look as if they just walked out of an ad for

Patagonia outdoor recreation clothing. Like Martha, even though we've just met, they let me in and hand over the keys to their home.

"We're happy to host you," says Brett, beaming. "Beth is so special to us, so we've been looking forward to meeting you."

Smiling, Ally agrees. "Yes, we're delighted to meet you, Kee Kee. You are welcome to stay as long as you like in the guest suite upstairs. It's very private and quiet up there with your own bathroom and sitting area."

"Thank you both for being so welcoming," I reply, as a small, fluffy black dog runs past and starts playing with Yoda. "Oooooh, and who is this adorable little guy?"

Brett laughs and says, "That's Turtle, and he seems quite smitten with Yoda."

Ally motions us into the kitchen. "I hope you're hungry for dinner because my homemade marinara sauce has been simmering on the stove for hours."

Uh, yes, please.

While we eat pasta and drink glasses of the traveling bottle of wine, I get to know them, and they are curious to hear more about Yoda and me on the road, going with the flow. Ally and Brett are warm, funny, and interesting. While they make me feel completely at home, Turtle spends hours nibbling on poor Yoda's ears, indicating that he'd like Yoda to stick around for a while. When I crawl into bed, a cozy contentment settles in. I've only known Ally and Brett for a few hours, yet I'm so comforted by feeling at home in their house.

Portland streets are filled with people on bikes, and they are riding them in the rain! When it rains in LA, things pretty much shut down. Southern Californians don't know how to deal with this weather because we rarely have it.

Growing up in Wisconsin, I loved the change of seasons, each bringing a new state of mind. Winter is a time to bundle up in oversized sweaters and connect with people through intimate conversation over hot beverages. Spring's flowering trees and daffodils pushing through the newly thawed ground deliver spring fever—that first day of warm weather after a long, cold winter when the sun is out, infusing everyone with joy. Summer brings lazy days usually centered on a lake: water skiing, boating, or sitting with a book in the shade of a tree beside the water. Then, my favorite season, the one that I've missed the most: autumn. The kaleidoscope of colors in the trees, the crunch of fallen leaves underfoot, the woodsy, earthy scent of piles of leaves, the smoky waft of bonfires, the sweet, juicy crunch of MacIntosh apples from my parents' yard, and freshly roasted pumpkin seeds, straight out of the oven. I'm happy to be visiting Portland in the fall.

Portland is a dog's paradise. Does everyone here carry dog treats in their pockets? Yoda has been having his fill of everything from smoked salmon and leftover filet mignon to homemade dog biscuits. I even find a doggie daycare where I check him in during the day while I explore the city.

One day, I have lunch with Justin, a high school friend and now a Portland State professor. I haven't seen him in twenty years, yet as we catch up over Indian food, it seems that no time has passed. Justin is newly married and recently underwent a career change from a high-profile C-suite executive position to becoming a philosophy professor. If he weren't so down-to-earth, I would be intimidated by his education and career path. He has an Ivy League education, with a PhD and Postdoc in neuroscience. Justin is a smart guy who ended up in the impressive place in life he was predicted to be, given our high school graduating class voted him "Most Likely to Succeed." He's pleased with his career path and choice to live in Portland.

I've subscribed to the definition of a successful life as having a reliable and secure career, owning a house, getting married, and having children. I don't have any of those things, and even if I did, would I be able to say that I've finally *succeeded?* Color me confused. Again.

Both Justin and Martha exude shama, and it doesn't escape me that their contentment might stem from living life in a way that embraces who they are instead of apologizing for who they are pretending to be. I wish I could live that way. I'm not pleased with where I am in my life, so I find Justin's reaction to my current situation quite curious. He could be appalled at what a failure I am, but instead, he's intrigued that I have just packed my life into my car and plan to keep driving until I figure out the changes I want in my life. Rather than thinking I'm crazy, Martha and Justin almost seem proud of me for driving headfirst into the unknown.

The light morning rain as we leave Ally and Brett's house doesn't seem like a big deal. However, as the drizzle becomes a deluge, the car briefly hydroplanes, and I cling fiercely to the steering wheel. I am as petrified as if I'm driving in a snowstorm. At times, the rain pounds so hard that I slow to a crawl because I can't see the car in front of me, which makes my heart beat in overdrive as my palms sweat in my iron grip on the wheel. I pull off the interstate at one rest stop and then another to collect myself before continuing the drive north into gradually clearing skies. I'm a founding member of the "I hate driving in the rain" club.

We arrive in Seattle just as the sun sets at the home of my friend Jesse from the backpack-less wedding adventure. She and her yellow lab welcome Yoda and me into a toasty, dry apartment. When she hands me a mug of hot green tea, I feel my shoulders drop with relief to be off the road.

The exhausting and stressful drive is worth it, because we wake up to the blessing of a crystal-clear Seattle autumn day with sparkling views of snow-capped Mount Rainier, the volcanic Cascade Range, and the Olympic Mountains. I am grateful for my time with Jesse in Seattle, where our non-stop activities distract me from the reasons behind my road trip, and it's almost as if I'm on vacation. We explore the city with our dogs, get coffees at the original Starbucks (that opened in 1971), wander around Pike Place Market (the nation's oldest farmers' market), and visit several outdoor cafes. We take photos of the Space Needle and hike with the dogs on a lush green trail.

After dinner on our last night in Seattle, we share glasses of the seemingly bottomless traveling bottle of wine. Although the V. Sattui Angelica is so rich that each serving tends to be little more than the size of a shot glass, it's baffling how a quarter of the bottle remains.

"Wait, how many people have you already shared this bottle with?" asks Jesse with amusement.

"It's wild," I laugh. "I'm starting to believe the bottle is enchanted and keeps refilling itself. A divine miracle, like the story of Jesus turning water into wine."

We reminisce about our adventures together on the recent Italy lost luggage backpacking trip, where, despite my attempts to live in the moment, everything reminded me of Harry.

I take a sip of wine and pull myself back into the conversation at Jesse's kitchen table.

"It's interesting, Jesse. Right now, being on the road, I'm feeling some of the same freedom I felt in Italy. You know, without my backpack."

"That sounds about right. If you have any hope of breaking out of your mental muck, you need to lose some life baggage," muses Jesse.

"So true. Princess Leia is a small car, which has forced me to travel light. As a result, my lack of *stuff* is making life less heavy."

"Here's to friendship, good wine, and to leaving the past behind," toasts Jesse as we clink glasses.

As we continue on the road, I pull into a rest stop to refill my travel mug with the free coffee that almost every rest area in the Pacific Northwest offers. Then, I take a short hike with Yoda through the pines behind the building while I snack on juicy, tart wild blackberries I pick along the way.

I may need to reframe the grief about losing Harry that I felt in Rome and am feeling now. It could be that Harry represents the closest I've ever come to having what I have always perceived to be the American dream.

If I'm successful in letting go of the past, then maybe I'm no longer running away from my life. As if the tectonic plates of my psyche have shifted, I'm beginning to think I might be running toward something. I'm not sure what that something is, but its call whispers my name. By leaving my baggage behind, I'm lighter and better able to listen to the voice of my intuition.

What a weighty lesson of the road. Travel light.

SIX

Bend

A friend has a vacation home in Sandpoint, Idaho, and has arranged for the caretaker to give me the keys. I'm looking forward to watching the sunrise over the lake with a steaming cup of coffee in my hand, taking long hikes with Yoda in the Rocky Mountains, and tasting Sandpoint's famous huckleberry preserves.

After Idaho, I've been planning to drive on some of the same roads in Montana that John Steinbeck drove with his dog Charley during their 1960 road trip across the United States. In the book *Travels with Charley*, Montana was the state to which Steinbeck proclaimed his love, and I want to experience for myself how Montana captured his heart. However, I checked the weather forecast this morning, and Northern Idaho is in for a snowstorm.

Despite learning to drive on winter roads in Wisconsin, I've primarily spent my driving years on LA's mostly weather-free roads. Traffic, yes; snow, never. Even after the demonstration from the mechanic at the garage where I had my taillight fixed, I doubt I could put snow chains on my tires. The thought of hitting ice and being unable to stop, fishtailing out of control, or, God forbid, even crashing brings a cold sweat. The image of ending my search for shama in a snowbank makes me shiver. So, driving in snow? No thanks.

Forget about it. I can't go to Sandpoint.

Once again, my plans have fallen through—something that's becoming a theme for this road trip. Yet the whole Ben disaster led to a marvelous, insightful adventure on Mount Hood, which led to spending a few lovely days with Ally, Brett, and Turtle in Portland, so there's something to be said about embracing the unknown, scary as it is. After all, isn't that the purpose of this quest? Serendipity may be the golden goose of road trips—finding what I didn't know I was looking for that I undeniably need.

A few hours ago, I phoned my dad, who has christened himself as my road trip travel agent. When I told him about the crappy weather, Dad spread out his maps and asked me how many hours I want to drive today. We decide together that I'll head to Central Oregon, which entails driving over Mount Hood. Despite the snowfall yesterday, today is a welcome sunny morning. The relentless rain of the trip is finally letting up again, at least for the morning hours. All I ask for is enough time to get across the mountain pass without any weather getting in my way.

When I open the car door, Yoda springs in and lands on his bed, standing on all fours. It's as if the anticipation of the unknown is his favorite part of the journey. We drive into the charming alpine village of Government Camp to fill Princess up with gas and my travel cup with java, and we pass a quaint coffee shop named Three Sisters, which gives me pangs of missing *my* three sisters. On the rare occasions that the four of us are together in the same place, I love curling up on the sofa with a warm mug of coffee and talking with them. We've laughed, cried, and gossiped together, and although we can debate with the best, we are sisters at the end of the day. It's a sacred thing, both being a sister and having a sister.

I'm never far from craving coffee, and it's not really about the taste or the caffeine buzz. What I love is the meditative ritual of exploring the sensory nuances of coffee—the burbling sound of the pouring liquid, the nutty aroma laced with notes of chocolate, and the soothing warmth of the mug as I cup it with both hands and hold it close to my chest. So, there's no question about what to do next. After U-turning Princess and parking the car, I walk into Three Sisters.

"Hi traveler, what can I get you?" asks the woman behind the counter, surrounded by so many choices of coffee.

"I'd love a cup of your organic Guatemalan."

The coffee shop is a tiny one-room wooden cabin that sells home-baked goods and hand-made crafts. As the barista pours steaming coffee into my travel mug (oh yeah, that's what I'm talking about), she asks where I'm headed.

"I'm driving over the pass for the first time, and I hope to arrive in Bend by early evening."

"Well, as long as you're in the area, you absolutely must drive five miles up the mountain to the Timberline Lodge," she insists.

Timberline, built in the 1930s, is a historical monument surrounded by the Mount Hood National Forest. It even served as the exterior of the Overlook Hotel in the movie *The Shining*.

"I had no idea it was around here," I exclaim. "However, I know you got a lot of snow yesterday, and I'd like to avoid driving on slippery roads."

After she assures me that the plowed road is ice-free, I drive up to explore. The mountain air is crisp, and the winter views are spectacular.

Yoda has a personal first at Timberline: snow. Yoda is a dog who is always channeling his inner cat. Constantly grooming himself, he would rather walk around a puddle than get his paws wet. It takes some bribery with treats to get him out of the slushy, plowed parking lot and into the half-foot of powdery white carpet that covers the lawn outside the lodge. When his paws first touch it, his eyes open wide, and he freezes mid-step. This Southern California dog is clearly not a fan of cold, wet, white stuff on the ground. Eventually, the combination of Yoda's pleading look ("Ma, get me outta here!") and my worries about getting to Bend before the rain or snow starts again makes me reluctantly leave within an hour of arriving. Before we climb back into the car, I close my eyes and inhale as slowly and deeply as possible to fill my lungs with the clean, cool mountain air. I am wide awake and full of hope.

We check into a small motel in Bend. The sun hasn't yet set, so I change into my swimsuit to soak my road-weary muscles in the outdoor hot tub on the edge of the parking lot next to the dumpsters. Ambiance is not something this hotel offers. Yet, at fifty-nine dollars a night, I can't complain. If the room is clean and I have free Wi-Fi, I can make myself at home almost anywhere. With Yoda tethered to the metal railing next to the tub, I whip off my sweats and quickly slip in. The air is cold, but the water is steaming hot. I close my eyes and melt as the jets blast my tight shoulder and neck muscles. My entire body is a bit achy, and my lymph nodes are tender. I've been fighting a cold since I got on the road and haven't quite kicked it. I'm tired from all the driving and need to rest. All I want to do is lie in bed and watch rom-coms.

But first: something to eat. I grab my towel, unhook Yoda's leash, and we run across the parking lot to the warmth of our room, where I change into dry clothes before we drive to a nearby grocery store for "dinner." I've figured out the formula for eating on the road. My plan is to stay in hotels and motels offering a free breakfast. Dinner is a different story. I rarely eat fast food, and my travel budget doesn't allow the luxury of dining in restaurants. Therefore, I'm becoming a fan of grocery store delis, where I hope to luck out and find something other than broccoli crunch salad and tuna salad drenched in copious amounts of mayonnaise. A favorite addition to my road trip dinners is sliced avocado and tomato with a sprinkling of sea salt flakes and cracked pepper. My strategy is to eat for under five dollars a meal. Tonight, my feast includes the mini jar of applesauce Martha gave me and a thinly sliced Honey Crisp apple from her neighbor's orchard with a piece of Swiss cheese.

One of my new road rules is to always request a mini fridge in my room. That way, I can keep my leftovers cold and eat them the next day. I'm traveling with a picnic backpack, so I can eat with proper plates and utensils, and then wash the dishes in my hotel sink. This little dinner ritual makes the hotel room feel more like home than eating from clamshell deli containers does. The backpack has an insulated cooler compartment to store cheese slices and bread so I can eat cheese sandwiches while driving. I fill Ziploc bags from the ice machine each morning to act as cold packs in the cooler. Another road trip discovery is a four-pack of single-serving bottles of wine. I can have one glass of wine with dinner to help melt any muscles that have tightened up from hours of driving and then stash the other three mini-bottles in my cooler to drink on future nights on the road. Oh yeah, I'm a quick learner about food and wine.

We end up staying four nights in Bend. Each morning, I request a late checkout, and then each afternoon, I walk into the front lobby and ask if I can stay one more night. Going forward, I won't drive more than three days in a row without taking a couple of days to regroup and rest.

Staying put in Bend is a happy accident. It's a gateway to the mountains and the high desert, a popular launching pad for both summer and winter sports. Autumn, well, not so much. Even so, we take long, lazy hikes daily along the mighty Deschutes River, and I pamper myself by sleeping in, taking naps, and binge-watching movies.

On our last day in Bend, Yoda and I drive to Smith Rock State Park. It's a place that Ally and Brett had mentioned was one of their favorite hiking spots. Grandiose rock spires overlook the windy Crooked River, and parts of the switchback trails allow for extraordinary views of the volcanic peaks of Oregon's Cascade Range. The terrain differs from what I have seen in Oregon so far; welded tuff (rock formed by volcanic ash), mystical rock formations, and sheer basalt cliffs make it one of the country's premiere climbing destinations. There's no one else on the trail, and it's so quiet that all I hear is the crunch from each step of my boots on the dirt path and the occasional soft snort when Yoda picks up a scent. Within the stillness of this dramatic high desert volcanic wonderland, I look around and see life everywhere.

I realize that everything in the world is alive, yet sometimes it takes the quiet solitude found in nature to feel the breath of Mother Earth. When a mossy rock captures my attention, I peer closely, my face inches from the green covering. What microscopic lifeforms call this cushiony kingdom their home? It pulsates with life force, so much so that I reach out and place my palm on it while saying a silent thank you to the Universe for creating such beauty on our planet.

The lace of rustling leaves on a nearby tree dances rhythmically. The tree speaks to me, and although I can't decipher its message, I'm comforted by its presence. In gratitude, I hug that tree like there's no tomorrow. Currents of grounding warmth and energy flow into my body as I surrender into the embrace.

With my eyes closed and my cheek pressed against the tree's deeply rutted bark, the quiet magic of nature rejuvenates my spirit. I have just learned my latest lesson of the road. Hello, tree. Hello, rocks. Hello, beautiful day.

SEVEN

Boise

It's late afternoon, and we're in Boise, Idaho. It's a place I don't know much about, and admittedly, somewhere that has never been on my radar to visit. I called Beth from my hotel in Bend and mentioned that I was taking a roundabout way to the Midwest to avoid the winter storm. After hearing that the route I was considering would go through Boise, Beth—who I'm convinced must know people in every nook and cranny of the U.S.—came through again and found a place for Yoda and me to stay. Her friend Shanti recently relocated to Boise from Los Angeles.

Shanti's home is a small, welcoming brick house with piles of colorful fall leaves in the yard. Yoda is eagerly whining—he's been in the back of the car for five and a half hours, after all—and once I leash him, he wastes no time jumping out and lifting his leg on the nearest tree. Shanti opens the door to greet us with an affable smile. I'm looking forward to getting to know another of Beth's friends. Shanti is renting out her spare bedroom, so we'll sleep on a blow-up mattress in the living room, and it's free.

After lugging in my bags, Shanti and I sit at the kitchen table with a couple of glasses of the traveling bottle of wine—that marvelous bottomless bottle—while Yoda gobbles up a bowl of kibble.

"Cheers to new friendships," I say, smiling.

We clink glasses.

"Beth told me you've started blogging," says Shanti.

"Yeah, I'm using an online template. Blogging helps me process the inner journey that I'm on. Plus, there's rarely cell reception on the road, and I'm usually too tired to have phone conversations at night after a day of driving, so it's a good way for family and friends to keep tabs on me."

Hmmm. I'm filled with excuses for avoiding conversations with most of my friends and family. Do I need to check out temporarily from the people of my past while I search out my future?

"I'm going to build you a pretty website to blog on that's easy to use." Shanti runs a business building websites.

"Really? You have time?"

"I can build it in a day, my gift for you. All you have to do is buy the domain name."

After we finish our wine (and make a second toast to my new website), Shanti whisks Yoda and me off to her friend's house, a short walk down the street, for more wine and homemade pickled vegetables with two friends from California.

Shanti is super cool, and meeting her is symbolic in a couple of ways. First, her name. "Shanti" in Sanskrit means "peace." That's what this road trip is all about—seeking shama and finding inner peace. "Shama" in Sanskrit means "peace and tranquility of the mind." The word sings to me like a lyrical ballad. The search for peace has been a lifelong journey for me. I even have a peace symbol tattoo that I got a few days after 9/11 as my small way to symbolize the world peace and inner peace that seemed impossible during that horrific week.

Second, tattooed on Shanti's forearm is my favorite quote about change, often misattributed to Gandhi, that originated in 1970 by Brooklyn, NY, teacher Arleen Lorrance: "You must be the change you want to see in the world."

I'm still following my mantra for this road trip—with every glance at the dashboard, the "I Welcome Change" sticky note reminds me. Okay, okay, Universe, I get it—I'm here for a reason.

The next morning, when we take Yoda for a walk, Shanti and I run into one of her artist friends. When she hears that Yoda and I are sleeping on an air mattress, she insists we stay at her charming boutique inn for free.

Our room is a cozy and artistically decorated suite with a kitchenette in a renovated historic 1895 home. It's decorated with the owner's original art, and the place radiates healing, cheerful energy. I am pleased to have a stove, and I'm craving greens, so I buy some organic kale at the local co-op and eat the entire head for dinner.

What would it be like to live somewhere other than the same Santa Monica triplex I've lived in for the past eight years? I loved the apartment when I moved in, but the energy turned stale over the years. I've been comfortably bored, yet with so many years of living there, it's too much trouble to move. I'd prefer the energy in my home to reflect the energy of the inn.

I don't have much time in the room over the next few days, because Shanti and her friends keep me busy with a whirlwind of activities.

We hike in Boise's scenic Rocky Mountain foothills and explore some cafes in the charming downtown area. To demonstrate that Boise has many available bachelors, Shanti lines up three coffee dates (all from an online dating app) for herself in one day and lets Yoda and me tag along. The guys get a kick out of Shanti making this part of my tour of Boise. Knowing my restrictions with Yoda's separation anxiety, Shanti takes us to a bar that welcomes dogs inside.

Shanti and her friends have all moved to Boise in search of a more affordable and better quality of life. When they learn how unhappy I am with my life in LA, they all make a pitch for me to move to Boise.

Amazingly, during my stay in Boise, I meet eight people through Shanti who have moved there from California, most from Los Angeles. Then, the day before I leave, when the Boise Toyota dealership fixes the flat tire(!) on Princess, I learn that six of the service people are also from California.

Boise must be a big remarkable secret that all Californians but me know about. After a few days there, I can already understand why people in the know would want to keep it under wraps: it's an affordable mixture of urban sophistication and outdoor playground, with a mild climate and small-town charm. A few months ago, the August 2010 issue of *Outside Magazine* named Boise the "best overall town in the western U.S."

Everyone is so dang jovial in Boise because they make a point to take a break in their lives and have fun. I'm impressed by the sense of community. The North End, where Shanti lives, is filled with professionals: doctors, lawyers, firemen, nurses, and entrepreneurs, and they all gather every six weeks for a themed party. For instance, in March, for the Sensory Illumination party, fire dancers and ceiling dancers entertain the costumed crowd in a warehouse. In June, the community enjoys three days of music and camping in the woods at the Esthetic Evolution party. December brings the Santa Rampage party, where everyone dresses up as Santa and elves and goes bar hopping through the city.

Shanti and her Boise crowd seem to realize that life is more than working long hours, as I've been doing. To them, it's about putting on false glittery eyelashes, feather boas, and crazy costumes, and having a good time to balance out their work lives. Although I doubt I could ever keep up with them, I admire their desire to have fun and forget about work now and then. These enthusiastic, fun-loving former Southern Californians are teaching me that there is indeed life after Los Angeles.

For my last morning in Boise, Shanti and I plan to visit a hot spring on my way out of town. Before we leave her house, Shanti, a flying yoga instructor, gives the perfect parting gift for a road tripper: partner yoga back traction. I've never heard of flying yoga, which combines traditional yoga and hanging from silky hammocks to allow for deeper stretches and decompression. Shanti tells me I will get the same benefit of "flying" with partner yoga. She instructs me to interlace my fingers behind my head. Then Shanti lies down with her back on the floor and places her feet at my inner hips and her hands on my elbows. She tells me to lean forward, let her legs and hands support my body, and have faith that she won't drop me. Slowly, she lifts and balances me above her while she gently pulls her feet and hands apart, leading to a blissful stretch of my spine. I imagine we look much like I did when I would lift my nephews in the air with my feet so they could "fly like Superman." I wonder if the Superman pose was this nurturing to them.

I'm intrigued that my stay in Boise ends with partner yoga. Being supported in the air by a partner's legs is an exercise in trust. Trust that she won't drop me. Trust that I won't fall on my head. Trust that I can let go of fear and be present in the moment, enjoying the stretch. Trust that this road trip will lead me to where I need to be. Trust that if I stay in the flow of the moment, I will eventually find the shama I am looking for. Trust is my latest lesson of the road.

EIGHT
Lava Hot Springs

Yoda and I will spend the rest of the week in Lava Hot Springs, Idaho. Although hardly a mineral spring connoisseur, I've been all over the world in search of them because soaking in the healing waters of a hot spring kick-starts my sleeping spirit, releases my gridlocked shoulder muscles, and quiets the traffic jam of my noisy mind. Many people expound on the health properties of steaming mineral water, such as offering relief for arthritis and digestive issues, providing speedy recovery to wounds, increasing blood flow and circulation, boosting metabolism, and allowing for absorption of essential minerals. The hot mineral water also leaves the body and soul relaxed and revived.

The long hours logged with Princess Leia the Prius are taking their toll on my shoulders, back, and hips, so I'm ready to indulge in the ultimate in self-pampering in a hot mineral spring. My favorite hot springs to visit are those hard-to-reach ones that take creative energy to locate. Directions might be "Park your car at mile marker four beside the river, then hike a mile up the hill on the unmarked trail until you hear the bubbling water." *Oh yeah, that's what I'm talking about.*

So, this morning, before Yoda and I leave the Boise area, I follow Shanti to one of those off-the-beaten-path springs about an hour outside of town. It's named Deer Creek Hot Springs, or, as the locals call it, Skinny Dipper Hot Springs. We hike up to one of the most beautiful springs I've visited, with three connected pools varying in temperature and size and a panoramic view of the Payette River.

After I tether Yoda to a tree, Shanti and I soak in all three pools. Our soak schedule is as follows: Soak in the hottest, smallest pool until our skin is red and beads of sweat break out on our upper lips. Move to the second hottest pool; take handfuls of the sandy bottom to exfoliate our skin. Move to the cooler, biggest pool to cool off, and then quickly move back to the second hottest pool when a family arrives and the kids start splashing around.

Unfortunately, Skinny Dipper Hot Springs isn't all relaxation. While attempting to take a photo, I step on a slick spot and have a major wipeout, leaving cuts and bruises where one should never have cuts and bruises. I also suffer from a compromised ego, since this event happens directly in front of the family with the splashing kids.

As I bleed and limp on the trek back down the hill with Shanti and Yoda toward our cars, I realize, "What better way to heal those cuts and bruises than to visit more hot springs?" Because, obviously.

Lava Hot Springs was originally a sacred gathering place for the Bannock and Shoshone Native Americans, who designated the area as neutral ground to be shared in peace by all tribes. The town now has a tiny population of about five hundred people. However, at the height of the summer tourist season, up to fifteen thousand people visit per month. Visiting during the off-season is a recurring theme for this road trip, meaning the town is quiet and peaceful when we arrive.

At the heart of Lava Hot Springs are the "World Famous Hot Pools," which consist of five mineral-laden, pebble-bottomed (acupressure for the feet, heavenly sigh) hot pools with temperatures ranging from 104 to 112 degrees Fahrenheit. Three million, five hundred thousand gallons of odor-free, naturally filtered water bubble out of natural underground springs and course through the pools every single day.

The next few days involve hours of soaking in the pools, which I have all to myself because it's the off-season. Luckily, Yoda's separation anxiety doesn't rear its ugly head when he's alone in the car. The weather is such that I can leave him with the windows open slightly without worrying about him getting too hot or cold. He either lies down and goes to sleep, or looks out the windows, calmly observing the world passing by, which means I can enjoy my soaks for over an hour without Yoda having a panic attack. That's a good boy.

I spend my days hiking in the nearby mountains with Yoda, then soaking at the World Famous Hot Pools, and then, after bringing back dinner from the local market's deli to eat in my room, I soak one more time in the mineral spring tub in my room before I melt into the mattress like a waterlogged blob of lavender putty.

The historic Home Hotel was built in 1918 and is the only hotel in the city with private jetted hot spring tubs in the rooms, a luxury I can't forgo. Yes, please. The water in the tub is the perfect temperature to counter the nocturnal chill of the outside air. Draping a hot, wet washcloth across my chest creates a sense of security, quelling the fight-or-flight response and providing a swaddling effect that helps me relax even deeper into the bath. Tiny bubbles float to the surface when I move my hand under the water. Where does the air come from that forms the bubbles?

Harry introduced me to the world of hot mineral springs. Visiting them was a shared passion that took us as far away as several secluded onsens in the mountains outside Tokyo. They gave us robes to wear all day when we weren't in the springs—heavy woolen ones for walking to the outdoors springs and lightweight cotton ones for indoors. While we were soaking in the afternoons, they converted our traditional tatami mat room into an intimate private dining room, with a dozen beautiful small plates of food on a low table. We sat on cushions on the floor with our crossed legs tucked under a blanket covering the table with a lightbulb underneath to keep us warm. While we were soaking after dinner, they cleared the table and rolled out the futons for sleeping. Yet as extraordinary as our international hot spring adventures were, some of our favorites to visit were close to home, a car ride away in Palm Springs, Desert Hot Springs, and San Luis Obispo.

My post-Harry hot spring discoveries have been bittersweet. Hot springing has become a part of my identity, and with each new experience, it's as if I've excavated another precious gemstone to add to my treasure chest of memories. However, no matter who I'm with or where I am, I wish Harry was there to discover it with me. Now is no exception.

I take a deep breath and slide my back down the tub so that my head's underwater, surrendering to the womb-like comfort of sensory deprivation. I hold my breath for as long as is comfortable before I come up for a big gulp of air. Yoda is sitting next to the tub, looking at me with a curious head tilt.

"Hey, big guy," I laugh as I reach for him, and he ducks away with fear that I'm going to get him wet. He leaps to the other side of the hotel room, grabs his stuffed animal coati toy, and madly shakes it back and forth. "Come on Ma, remember me? Playtime."

Watching him play brings a wistful smile. If Harry and I were together, I wouldn't have adopted my dog, since Yoda and

I found each other when I was reeling from a different breakup. I wouldn't be taking this road trip right now, meeting so many interesting people and discovering all these wonderful places, like Lava Hot Springs, a city I never knew existed until a few days ago. Oh, my goodness, if I was still with Harry, would we be stuck in the cycle of him being afraid of commitment and me insecure about being myself, trying to be the type of woman he could love? Was the reality Harry and I shared as wonderful as what I've been missing?

Now that Yoda has shamed me out of my water reverie, I climb out of the tub and wrap my hair in a thick, plush, white towel, and my body in another. Yoda jumps on the bed and circles four or five times before finally lying down and closing his eyes with a soft groan. I whisper, "I love you, Yoda." I am exactly where I want to be right now.

Although the Lava Hot Springs mineral pools are the nicest commercial hot springs I've ever visited, I discover the most memorable part of this small town through a conversation with Trevor, the front desk clerk at my hotel. Trevor grew up in Lava Hot Springs, yet unlike most town folk, with his numerous piercings and tattoos, he carries a unique energy. I find him intriguing—young and itching to explore the world. Yoda and I visit with him a handful of times in the lobby, with the excuse that I want some of the free hot coffee they always have brewing.

"Are there any secret hot springs in the area that only the locals know about?" I ask him during one such visit.

He pauses briefly and then gives me an impish smile. "A spring bubbles up next to the Portneuf River and flows into it. The locals call it Chicken Soup Hot Springs because, legend has it, women in the 1920s would put their chickens in the hot waters to help with plucking feathers."

"Ewww! But seriously, how close is it, and how do I get there?"

"It's very close. Walk through the RV park, climb over the big boulder at the back of the lot, and then walk along the riverbank until you see steam rising."

Early the next morning, Yoda and I find Chicken Soup Hot Springs for me to enjoy a private soak as the sun rises. Of course, I'd be lying if I say the soak is pure relaxation. You see, during that same conversation with Trevor, he told me about another local legend: ligers. Ligers are that mythical hybrid of a lion and tiger that the title character in *Napoleon Dynamite* so loved. At least, I thought they were mythical until an Internet search revealed that in 1995, two people were convicted of animal cruelty after ligers escaped from Ligertown, an illegal exotic game ranch near Lava Hot Springs.

Trevor swears ligers still live in the hills around Lava Hot Springs, but their existence is kept under wraps so as not to disturb tourism. Although the authorities claim they either captured or killed all the ligers from Ligertown, Trevor says the locals still have occasional sightings. His stories are convincing. And scary. While attempting to soak in Chicken Soup Hot Springs, I can't stop thinking of the large piles of animal scat next to the river. They could be from elk, deer, moose, bobcats, or even a horse—or ligers. With that thought, I'm officially freaked out, and I climb out and quickly throw on my clothes. Yoda and I bolt back to the safety of the hot spring tub in my room. No ligers here.

During this one last soak, it dawns on me that I'm letting go of the anxiety and baggage I have carried with me for years. The stress, self-imposed as it may be, has been a heavy load.

Changes seem to be happening within me daily, although I can't yet quite define them. While it's a lonely process, this road trip is helping me get to know myself better.

Native Americans considered hot springs sacred, where the "Great Spirit" lives, and thus believed that the waters were a place where miraculous healings could occur. The thing about soaking in mineral-rich hot springs, especially alone, is that I get philosophical and spend time thinking about life, love, and nothing at all. Perhaps it's only when one releases control and surrenders to the "nothing" part that healing transformation has room to happen.

Taking the time to be present as I soak in the hot thermal waters calms the confusion and crazy in my life and opens room for healing my mind and spirit. The takeaway isn't about luxuriating in hot springs all day (although I highly recommend it)—the lesson of the road is to take time, actually *make* time, to *just be.*

NINE

Salt Lake City

Last year, my childhood friend Heidi found me on Facebook. We met in Iowa when my family moved in next door to her family. Being the same age—four—it was a given that we'd become best friends. Our memories include dressing in costumes and charging a nickel for the grown-ups to watch our dance routines, sitting in a tree in my front yard, and arguing about whose dad was stronger. We played hard, and we fought hard. She even bit me once. I told on her.

A few years later, our family moved to Wisconsin, and we eventually lost touch as time passed—until she found me on Facebook. Now that I know she lives in Salt Lake City, Utah, Yoda and I can visit when the snowstorm changes our route. I meet her husband, Blane, and their enchanting four-year-old daughter, Hope.

The magic that made our childhood friendship so special is still there between us. We marvel that she's a mom with a daughter the age we were when we met. Heidi takes me downstairs to the finished basement and the guest bedroom, where Yoda eagerly leaps onto the bed.

"Yoda is allowed on the bed," she says, kissing his head.

I grab the memory foam pillow and hug it to my chest. "I'm so excited to have a good pillow for once. My neck is killing me from all the bad hotel pillows."

Heidi smiles and says, "It's yours. Take it with you."

I appreciate this great news because I didn't consider bringing my pillow on the road.

Hope runs into the room wearing a lavender princess costume and holding a fistful of colorful quills. She squeezes her eyes shut and crinkles her freckle-splashed nose as she eagerly squeals, "Mommy, let's show her the feathers."

We sit on the floor and spread the feathers out in front of us, which Yoda promptly begins sniffing. Heidi, an aviculturist, tells us what birds they come from. Hope looks up at her mom with awe and pride in her eyes.

Hope stands up and, with a swish, twirls in a circle, making her tulle skirt billow around her.

I laugh with delight and tell her, "Hope, when your mom and I were your age, we always played dress-up. We'd put on wigs and dresses that our moms wore in the 1970s."

Heidi looks at me with twinkling eyes and says, "I have a surprise for you."

She opens the closet door in my guest bedroom and pulls out two plastic tubs filled with wigs and some of the old clothes we used to dress up in. An impromptu dress-up party ensues. I throw on a bright pink wig and a metallic blue dress with a red feather boa, and Heidi wears a big flowered hippie dress with a long blue wig. Blane comes into the room and snickers when he sees us, then throws on a curly wig and a Count Dracula-style black cape with red lining. He stands over Hope's small electronic keyboard and plays spooky music. Hope sits on the floor with Yoda and giggles at us. We're all chuckling at how goofy we look, and my belly is sore from laughing harder than I have all year. It feels good.

"Let's give the chickens an afternoon snack," says Heidi to Hope, referring to her flock of chickens that roam around the fenced-in backyard.

"How about I watch from inside?" I suggest, suddenly timid and no longer laughing.

My fear of chickens began when I was a toddler. I was *terrified*, even though, in reality, I had never seen a chicken. One day, my dad brought home his bounty from a hunting trip and placed a dead pheasant into my arms that I petted like a baby doll. He told me it was a chicken, which cured my fear—until we moved in next door to Heidi in Iowa.

Heidi's family raised a flock of chickens, including a temperamental rooster. I vividly remember sitting on my tricycle in the driveway watching Heidi run by screaming, followed seconds later by the angry, squawking rooster. Even though a chicken never pecked me, I've carried this irrational fear into adulthood.

On the one hand, Heidi having chickens is thrilling, because she makes toad-in-the-hole for breakfast with freshly laid eggs. There is something so satisfying about cracking open colorful speckled shells over a sizzling frying pan just minutes after Hope collects eggs from the nests.

On the other hand, I am alarmed: *chickens are roaming free in the yard.* Everyone has their demons. For me, it's ligers and chickens. The irony of being chicken of chickens is not lost on me. Especially these birds. The four chickens are friendly and affectionate. They follow Heidi around the yard and nuzzle up to her.

Determined to help me face my fear, Heidi drags me outside the next day.

I'm breathless, digging in my heels.

"Kee Kee, meet Charlotte, our sweetest chicken." She plops Charlotte right into my arms.

Heh heh, I'm holding a chicken. Look at that beak. You'd think I was holding a hawk. I wouldn't be as scared of a hawk. *Can chickens smell fear?*

"She loves to be stroked on her back. Try it. You might like it as much as she does. Her feathers are soft," she says gently, coaxing me.

Eventually, I pet Charlotte on the back. Charlotte couldn't be more accommodating, even though I can't hand her back to Heidi fast enough. Later, I also try, for all of two seconds, to participate in feeding the flock their mid-afternoon snack of carrots and bread, but the fear of being pecked on the hand makes me quit almost before I start. I know it's irrational, but it's real for me.

Later that evening, Blane starts a bonfire in the fire pit, and we head outside to make s'mores. As I pour the final glasses of the traveling bottle of wine, I feel it's fitting to be with my most longtime childhood friend when we finally drain the magic bottle.

As we're nursing the last drops of the wine in our glasses, I fess up to my second secret fear: driving in the snow. No, this irony is not lost on me either—I learned to drive in winter weather when living in Wisconsin. For this reason, I tell them I'm cutting my visit short because of the snow forecast later in the week, and I want to ensure that Yoda, Princess, and I clear the mountain pass before even a speck of weather is present.

The following morning, after we say our goodbyes, it starts hailing as I begin to pull out of the driveway. That's not in the forecast. Heidi reassures me through the car window that it's typical in Salt Lake City for precipitation to happen for a few minutes and then stop.

Except not always. Apparently. And not this time.

When Yoda and I arrive in the mountain pass, the rain turns to snowflakes and sleet. For an average driver, the weather isn't too awful. Who said I'm an average driver? Fortunately, even though the snow accumulates on the hood of my car and visibility is low, it melts the minute it hits the freeway. Nevertheless, my worst fear has materialized: I'm driving the mountain pass in a snowstorm with no way to turn back. Freeway signs instruct slow-moving vehicles to flash their hazards, and I move to the far-right lane. In my mind, I hear Heidi's reassuring voice telling me that when driving in snow, "Don't think about what other drivers think or say about your driving. Go as slow as you need to feel in control." For me, that is *super-duper slow*—a snail's pace.

With great relief, I eventually make it over the mountain pass. In the snow. Navigating the moment in a comfortable way without comparing myself to other people on the road. Isn't that how we should do things in life? Do we ever need to compare ourselves to those on the other side of the fence (or road)?

I can't say I've conquered my fears of chickens and driving in the snow. But I have faced them and survived. That feels damn good. Yoda, of course, expected no less. I imagine he thinks, "I knew you could do it."

Facing my fears is simple, like my willingness to hold a chicken and drive in a snowstorm, or complex, like leaving my life behind and taking a long road trip in search of a better tomorrow. The lesson of the road is to look fear in the eye and say, "I am not going to let you control my life. Dammit."

TEN

Cheyenne

The snow continues, and although I'm patting myself on the back for my mountain pass bravery, I'm not feeling enlightened. *Buddha-nature, where are you when I need you?*

I'm trying hard not to hyperventilate as I drive. My hands are shaking, there is a muscle spasm in my neck, and my bloodshot eyes are pinprick dry from not blinking for fear of looking away from the snowy road for even a second. *Please. Stop Snowing!* It's curious how just when you think you're getting a handle on things, a momentary crisis hits, your composure and peaceful vibes disappear, and you want to curse out God for—ya know, whatever. I'm a freakin' wreck. Oops, it's not a good time to say "wreck." At least I've finally cleared the mountain pass and crossed into Wyoming. So, there's that. A tear of frustration leaks out.

It was bound to happen at some point during this road trip. The only surprise is that it has taken a month. I'm talking about my road trip meltdown—where I question my sanity for deciding to take on a trip of this magnitude alone. It's more than the physical travel—it's the mental and emotional journey, untethered from all that is familiar: my routine, my neighborhood, my friends, my home. I want to crawl into bed and pull the covers over my head to avoid facing the universal truths that inevitably present themselves as my thoughts go into overdrive during long, lonely stretches on the highway. It's the

89

classic hoodwink—all sunshine and lollipops until I hit a bump in the road (like a snowstorm!), and then the traffic cam filter recalibrates to doom and gloom.

A flush crawls up my neck. How did I think that driving around the country alone without a plan would help me create change in my life and find shama in my heart? As I eye the snowbanks lining the highway, even my dashboard sticky note can't convince me I'm doing the right thing.

"Come on, Yoda, talk me off the ledge. It's not that bad, right?" Some enlightenment. Some higher place. Not me, not now.

Yoda watches the road ahead from the back seat and doesn't talk back.

Until now, I've spent a lot of time with people, friends old and new. In many ways, I have been pretending to myself that I'm on holiday. It has been easy to get lost in socializing, ignoring the real reason for my road trip. Yet now, with many solitary days of driving ahead of me, the reality of my situation hits hard: this is no vacation; this is a bona fide existential crisis.

I am having deep conversations with Princess Leia, the car, and Yoda, the dog, about the state of my life, and it's clear that my two travel companions, who are not human, will not give me the answers I seek—only blank looks.

"Yoda, I promise to take care of you always, no matter where we are. But *where* will we end up after this? Where should we go if we leave LA for good, and what will I do for work?"

In the rearview mirror, I see Yoda watching me as if he's listening closely.

"Princess, I'm lonely. I miss Harry. Why can't I stop thinking about him? Why did he have to surface right before we left LA? Why did he have to plant the seeds of *what if* in my head?"

Princess hums along, wheels rolling on the pavement stretching out ahead of us.

"Princess and Yoda, will I ever find shama?"

Yoda yawns.

I turn up the volume on my iPod when the song by my friend Rick Kurek, "One of Those Years," comes through on the rotation of my road trip playlist:

Friend, won't you save my soul
Cause I'm out of control
I'm staring at my liver
At the bottom of a goldfish bowl
So won't you save my soul
Let me get a few more beers
'Cause it's been one of those days,
one of those weeks, one of those years

Rick wrote the song when he was on a road trip himself. He was sitting under a freeway underpass while he wrote it, feeling alone and questioning where his life was going. I get it. I'm sitting alone under my metaphorical underpass. I have always loved the truth in the lyrics, but now, this song has a special meaning. I hear ya, Rick.

It's strangely comforting to pass through the otherworldly rock formations along the river when driving through Green River, Wyoming. The day probably would turn out better if I took the time to stop and explore what looks like a marvelous outdoor recreational area. However, we still have over seven hours of driving ahead, and it's now raining. Hard. At least it's not snowing, which is something to be thankful for. So onward we drive.

Eventually, the rain turns to a devouring wind. Like Boreas, the Greek god of the icy north wind, carrying off a protesting Oreithyia, will Princess be picked up and flung through the air? When we cross the Continental Divide, a sharp stab of loneliness cuts so deep I swear it draws blood—at this point, we've been driving for over an hour without seeing one other car.

Checklist: Cold. Rainy. Windy. Miserable. Heartbroken. Lonely. Where the hell am I? It's as if someone (is that you again, Universe?) is trying to prove to me that, yes, in this world, we are truly alone.

It's no wonder I have the road to myself. Although Wyoming is the tenth-largest state by area, it's the smallest by population. With only six people residing per square mile in Wyoming, 2,344 people reside per square mile in LA. In 2009, the U.S. Census Bureau reported a Wyoming state population of only 544,270 people, whereas three times that many people live in the 13-mile-long span of Manhattan, not including the other NYC boroughs.

About two hours from my overnight stop in Cheyenne, I pull into a rest stop to walk Yoda. The only other vehicle at the stop is a silver pickup truck with California license plates. The parking lot is empty, so I can take any parking spot I want. I can even take up three spots by parking sideways. However, out of loneliness, I pull in beside the empty truck. I keep glancing back as Yoda and I wander about because I want to see the owner. Seeing another human being will bring comfort. Besides, it's wild to see my Prius with California plates parked next to a pickup truck with California plates, both silver, both sitting somewhere in the middle of the vast emptiness of Wyoming.

The insistent wind is cold, tempting me to load Yoda back into the warmth of the car, but I don't. Instead, we linger outside near the vehicles, hoping to see the other driver.

Soon, a man appears, rewarding our wait. He's clad in a mishmash of shorts, a Patagonia jacket, and Ray-Ban sunglasses, with a ponytail peeking out of a cowboy hat made of camouflage print. He has a cup of steaming coffee from the vending machine in one hand, and, in the other, a giant yellow lizard with a beard of spikes under its chin.

Seeing him and his pet is so random that, without thinking, I excitedly sputter, "Is that a bearded dragon?"

"Yeah, do you want to pet it?"

I may be afraid of chickens, but I readily reach out and touch the reptilian scales on its back, which are much softer than I expect. Setting his coffee on the truck's roof, the man scratches Yoda behind the ears. When we start talking, he seems as grateful as I am to see another human being. Our stories are nearly identical.

Nodding at his truck, I say, "California plates, huh? Me too. I'm from LA. Where are you from?"

"I lost my job in Santa Cruz and don't know what I want to do next. So, I loaded up the truck, and I'm heading to the Midwest to visit family."

Instead of a dog, his travel mate is his pet bearded dragon, now lounging contentedly in the newly returned sunshine on his dashboard.

"I also lost my job, and the only thing I could think to do was drive. I'll visit my family in Wisconsin at some point," I say.

"I'll probably leave California permanently and live with my parents while I find a new job," he says with a wistful look.

"California felt like the place where dreams would come true when I first moved there," I lament. "But that never happened for me. I'm ready for something different, but I don't know where I would move, or what I would do if I left the film business."

A gust of wind flips the brim of his hat, and he reaches up to pull it snugly onto his head. "How is your car handling this weather?"

"I wasn't happy about driving in the snow over the Utah mountain pass, but luckily it wasn't too bad. However, this wind is next level." I pull my jacket tighter around me.

"I must have been about thirty minutes behind you, because the snow was bad enough that I had to stop and put chains on the tires of my truck. How did I beat you here?"

"I've taken driving breaks a couple of times to walk Yoda, so you must have passed me during one of those stops."

He tilts his head to point to his bearded dragon. "It sure makes traveling less lonely to have our pets riding shotgun, doesn't it?"

"Oh yes. I'm so grateful Yoda is with me. We're having adventures that become part of our shared story. These memories belong just to the two of us."

"There's something sacred about that," he says, as he takes a sip of his coffee before putting it in the truck's cupholder.

As if to agree, Yoda whines and then looks toward Princess. He's ready to get going.

I'm intrigued by having such a heartfelt conversation with a stranger when we're only briefly connecting, as we're both driving alone on the open road after our lives became unsustainable in California. If we weren't smack dab in the middle of nowhere, I'd invite him to share a meal, since misery loves company. Instead, I wish him luck, and, with a wistful smile, Yoda and I pile back into Princess.

These little gems can happen while driving into the unknown. For a moment, listening to another human being, I walk in their shoes, and get a vibe of their life. Our interaction gives me a lift and relief from my relentless thoughts of doom and gloom. For a few minutes, it reminds me that I'm not alone and what I experience isn't unique.

Yoda and I arrive at a small remote hotel in Cheyenne just after sunset. After checking into my room, for the first time on my road trip I break out my prized bottle of Don Julio 1942. I packed it on a whim, not thinking I would ever open the expensive, buttery, exquisite bottle of tequila that a friend gave me as a bon voyage gift. After today's drive, though, a shot of tequila feels necessary. I find a shrink-wrapped disposable cup next to the sink in my room, add ice from the hallway ice machine, and pour a shot. Then I log onto the hotel's Wi-Fi and check my email. Like a flashing neon light screaming READ ME FIRST, a message from Harry jumps out. Heart racing, I click on it.

He doesn't say much, only, "I hope your travels are going well. When do you get back? I'd like to see you."

Why does he want to see me? I wish he would tell me more and not be so cryptic. I want to know if he and his wife are getting a divorce. Why won't he leave my head and heart (or his wife)? This question is going to circle in my brain for days.

Today's driving has drained me of emotion, and I can't possibly respond to his email. So, I close my laptop, curl up with Yoda on the tacky floral polyester bedspread on one of the two queen beds, and flip on the TV. I intend to spend the evening locked in a lover's embrace with my glass of good ol' Don.

Then, my cell phone rings. I've welcomed the terrible cell reception on the road because it gives me an easy excuse for why I can't (or don't want to) return missed calls and must email people back instead. Rightly or wrongly, I need to distance myself from people while trying to get more in touch with myself.

When I see it's Beth calling, though, I want to answer. As I ramble on to her about questioning the soundness of my decision to take a long road trip by myself, I sip tequila and close my eyes to hold in tears.

"What have I been thinking, Beth? Who does this sort of thing? Now here I am alone in the middle of Wyoming with a bottle of tequila next to me and no idea how my actions can help me." Looking into my cup, I jiggle the ice. "I'm certainly not going to find shama by chasing it down the neck of a tequila bottle."

Beth is the world's best listener. She hears the important things in between the words I speak and often understands what I'm trying to articulate before I do. Then she explains it to me.

"You know, you aren't alone on your journey. Your family and friends are there with you every step of the way. Physically spending time alone in the car, well, that's your choice," she says, and her voice consoles me. "Your loved ones were there before your trip, and we will be there for you after. During your trip, we're all praying that you figure things out and will be happy again soon."

This call with Beth is what I needed.

All I can think is *I've chosen to be alone. Why?*

All I can say is "Thank you."

We hang up the phone, and I stare at my plastic cup of tequila. While Beth's words ring true, I don't know what to do with them.

I've lost interest in alcohol, so I dump it down the drain and leash Yoda for a pre-bedtime walk around the hotel parking lot.

The drive to North Platte, Nebraska, is so flat that I imagine I can see from one end of the state to the other. My dad and I drove through Nebraska in March of 1996 when he was helping me move to LA, and from our boredom with the flat terrain came one of the peak experiences of my life: tens of thousands of sandhill cranes migrating north for the summer along the North Platte River. The ground and the sky were black with a blanket of these majestic birds, and we were in awe at the sight. Given November is the month sandhill cranes usually make an overnight stop in North Platte on their way south for the winter, we're staying in North Platte so that I can turn this dark, lonely stretch of my road trip around by getting another fix of these magnificent birds.

We drive for two hours around North Platte to all the spots I've read about to find the birds. Yet I don't spot a single sandhill crane. I am utterly dejected. After stopping to pick up dinner at a nearby market, I take Yoda back to our hotel room, intending to make microwave popcorn and break out reliable Don for the second night in a row. But wait. Last night's call from Beth was a lifesaver. Might feeling lost and alone be an important part of my journey? Maybe I need this time alone to process what I have been through, to grieve the life I am leaving, and to dream up a healthy new life. Beth's call reminded me that my friends and family still love me and will always be there for me. *I am not alone.* It's another tough one, but that is my latest lesson of the road.

I don't need Don Julio for company. I have Yoda. Besides, tequila tastes better when you share it with friends.

ELEVEN

Eldon

Pie Heals. Pie is comfort food. Pie makes people happy. I've been hearing these bits of wisdom from Beth for years now. Since this road trip is all about healing, it's a no-brainer that I should visit her and put her nuggets of wisdom to the test—and eat pie.

A few months ago, Beth was a pie judge at the Iowa State Fair and, somehow or another, decided to move from LA into the American Gothic House, the little white farmhouse in the background of Grant Wood's iconic 1930 painting *American Gothic*. It's the most parodied painting in the world, of the stern-looking farmer (modeled after the Wood family's dentist) holding a lethal-looking pitchfork, standing next to a woman modeled after Wood's sister. The historic home featured in the painting is in Eldon, Iowa. I never even knew the house was real. Beth plans to bake pies there and write a memoir about the healing power of pie. Crazy, right? Not for Beth.

She is a pie whisperer, internationally famous for her pie blog, theworldneedsmorepie.com. The thing about Beth is she's the real deal. She believes in her heart of hearts that pie heals, and she is living proof of the power of pie. About a year ago, Beth's husband unexpectedly passed away from a ruptured aorta. In one short moment, life as she knew it shattered, and Beth became a widow. Her grief was deep, and her searing pain palpable. I'm sure she was tempted to crawl into bed and stay there for all eternity. Worse, she admits that she didn't want to keep living. Instead, thankfully, she dove headfirst into the world of pie.

Beth's passion for travel takes a close second to her passion for pie, so to jump-start her healing, she combined the two and hopped in her late husband's RV to travel the country and explore pie. Through her tears on the road, she baked pie, ate pie, continued to write about pie and her grief, and gave away free pie. At one point, Yoda and I joined her for a weekend at California's Faria Beach, where we baked a cherry pie in the RV's oven. Then, we spent the weekend eating slices during various conversations about her late husband that had us either in fits of laughter over her stories about him or spilling buckets of tears over her devastation about losing him.

Over the past fourteen months, Beth has been learning to cope with her loss and is slowly coming back to life. She understands how the open road can heal the heart and has been hugely instrumental in giving me the courage to take this extended road trip alone. Beth inspired me with her example of her time on the road in her RV and her encouraging words about life after loss—and after Los Angeles. I need to work up the courage to find that life. Beth knows far too well how challenging living in LA can be, since she periodically calls the City of Angels her home. She also understands sorrow and the healing process. She is an emotional rock for me as I work to restore health to my battered and bruised spirit. I need my friend, so her new home is my next stop on the road.

Along the way, I add to my road trip rules. A new one is that although I don't need to know where I will be in two days, I do need to know where I will end up that evening. As a single woman traveling alone, it seems safer to plan an overnight stop instead of driving around at the end of the day, hoping I'll find a safe, clean, dog-friendly hotel. One of my first rules—not to drive in the dark—is for safety, because after LASIK surgery to correct my vision seven years ago, I see halos and starbursts around bright lights (like headlights and taillights) at night. These halos and starbursts are not the groovy kind, unfortunately.

I am so excited to get to Beth's house that I break my rule not to drive in the dark. After a brutal nine hours on the road, I arrive after sundown, partly because of an almost thirty-minute traffic jam caused by a slow-moving tractor on a two-lane highway. While frustrating, the farm road bottleneck was a million times better than the gridlock on six-lane freeways in Los Angeles. Driving in the dark in the country adds an entirely new dimension of stress. One must always be on the lookout for deer that could run into the road at any moment, but it's all worth it once I park Princess and look up at the celebrated white American Gothic House.

The little girl in me widens her eyes and catches her breath while silently squealing, *I get to stay in a dollhouse!*

Before I have a chance to get out of the car, Beth runs out, hands me a glass of wine, and promptly informs me that we'll be getting up bright and early to make apple pies. She runs her new pie business, Pitchfork Pie Stand, out of the American Gothic House each Friday, Saturday, and Sunday.

When I first walk into the house and drop my bags, Beth gives me a knowing smile. "You can stay as long as you like, provided you abide by two house rules. The first is that you must read for thirty minutes each day. The second rule is that you're required to unpack."

"I'm totally on board with the reading rule, but your unpacking rule makes me uneasy."

Unpacking represents staying put, settling in, not running. The preoccupation with running away from my life may have led to my forgetting about living each moment of my life. Now. Not in the past and not in the future—living life in the present. Right now. Today. And that involves unpacking.

True to her word, the next day, after morning lattes and a dog walk through the neighboring soybean field, she puts me to work peeling Granny Smith apples for the pies. As we work side by side, me peeling apples and Beth assembling the pies, our conversation grows more and more quiet. Eventually, we stop talking altogether. Solely focused on peeling each apple with one long continuous knife cut, I watch the green peel curl, hang, and grow longer. Our work is very meditative. *Om mani padme hum*—it's Zen apple peeling therapy.

The apple peeling helps me accomplish what is often so difficult: letting go of the merry-go-round in my head and being present. Soon, I'm lost in the flow—the action is so soothing; I don't want to stop. A neighbor has dropped off a bushel of pears from her tree, so I tackle the huge basket and make pear sauce while the pies are baking. A potpourri of cinnamon, ginger, and vanilla lingers in the air of the kitchen: pear sauce simmering on the stove, alongside fresh-out-of-the-oven apple crumble pie, apple pie, and pecan pie. The aroma stirs hunger from somewhere beyond my stomach—a longing for the warmth and familiar comfort that I always found in my grandmother's kitchen.

I feel nourished by my time in Beth's kitchen—precisely what I need. I love the creative cooking process, and being on the road, I've missed it, even though I haven't had much time for cooking before. Little Miss Career Girl spent long hours working, and at the end of the day, was more apt to grab dinner from the Whole Foods deli than to spend time cooking. If I did cook, I'd be eating at 9 p.m. What a life. It's another reminder that leaving LA was a good thing—a healthy choice.

The initial idea is to stay with Beth for two nights, but, like most other plans on this road trip, I quickly scrap that idea. Living in one of the country's most famous residences is a peaceful, healing experience. Plus, there's pie.

After our morning baking pies in the kitchen, my belongings are still secure in my duffle bag—just in case.

Beth approaches me. "You've got this, Kee Kee. I've cleared out this tiny coat closet for you. Now get to work."

I groan.

Knowing the way to my heart, she hands me one of her famous lattes. "Take your time."

So, I do. I take each item from my large duffle bag and hang most on hangers. I line my shoes up in a row, neatly fold T-shirts and panties and tuck them in the corner of the closet. Iowa first delivered *Zen apple peeling therapy*, and now we have *Zen unpacking therapy*. Sitting on my haunches, I take a sip of my foamy latte and look at my tidy little closet. How do I feel?

Until now, the longest I stayed in any location was four nights. I have become oddly comfortable living like a drifter, shoving my belongings in their appointed corners of my duffle bag and only wearing the garments I randomly grab from the top layer. By unpacking, I have unearthed clothing I completely forgot about. I've had more important things to think about—like snowstorms, ex-boyfriends, a very needy dog, and wondering when the hell I'm ever going to find shama.

Discovering all my unused clothes doesn't matter. After unpacking, Yoda, Beth, and I head over to a Tractor Supply store.

I buy a John Deere bandana for Yoda and a pair of denim bib overalls for myself—from Hollywood exec to vagabond to Iowa farm girl. Proudly, Yoda and I wear our new Iowa clothing every day at Beth's. To ensure I'll stay awhile, Beth sets up an ironing board as a makeshift desk for me, with a view out the back Gothic window. While it's identical to the Gothic window at the front of the house in the celebrated painting, it overlooks the backyard. I can't imagine a more inspiring place to read and write (or iron). I spend hours each day sitting at my desk, typing blog posts about my journey on the new website that Shanti built for me, and daydreaming while gazing out of that wonderful, marvelous Gothic window.

However, what speaks to me louder than the famous Gothic window or the wildly surreal fact that I am sleeping in the American Gothic House, is the simple country life. While I'm still in bed the second morning, Beth introduces me to everyday rural living.

I open my eyes to see her standing over me in her bathrobe, holding a bird that isn't moving.

"I found it lying on the ground outside the back door."

Struggling to shake the fog of sleep, I remember that Beth recently rescued an orphaned baby bunny during a bike ride. Sadly, the bunny didn't make it, leaving Beth wrecked and triggering the grief she is trying to put behind her. Now, here she is with a little bird in her hands. This bird needs a happy ending.

I climb out of bed and look at the bird. "I think it's stunned. It must have hit the window."

Beth and I spring into action. Well, Beth is springing. I stumble in my groggy stupor.

"Grab that Tupperware container," Beth says as we walk through the kitchen to head outside. "Let's fill it with dried grass and twigs to make a nest."

We place the bird in our hastily made nest and suspend it from the clothesline in the backyard, out of reach of our dogs, and we stand on guard, watching, praying, and willing that bird to move. Finally, we leave it alone. An hour later (after drinking one of Beth's lattes), we return just in time to see it fly away. Today is getting off to a good start. We've already saved a life and haven't even had breakfast.

The autumnal sunset lights the clouds ablaze, with an inferno of orange and pink rays of light illuminating the street as we walk Yoda with Beth's terriers, Jack and Daisy. We pass the local "kennel," which consists of a wretched outdoor chain-link cage where the town puts stray animals.

Beth gestures toward the cage. "Welcome to the saddest part of this small town. If animals are unclaimed after three days, they euthanize them."

Jeepers.

A skinny yellow lab with a cloudy left eye sits in the back of the cage, quivering. When he sees us, he gives a half-hearted wag of his tail.

The sight breaks my heart. "Oh, the sweet thing. He looks as if he hasn't eaten in weeks. The poor guy has no food or water in the cage."

"Look at the trash and dirty old tarp cluttering the floor. Come on, people! That's no way to treat an animal!" cries Beth.

Since the cage is padlocked, Beth and I do what we can to make the starving dog's last hours comfortable. While Beth runs back to the American Gothic House to get supplies, I hold our three dogs' leashes and send good vibes to the lab, who seems to appreciate the company. "Here are some dried chicken snacks for you." I throw a couple of handfuls of Yoda's treats into the cage while praying for the lab's survival. Mistreated animals hit me in the gut.

When Beth returns, she slides a plastic bowl filled with water into the cage. "Drink up, big guy."

Later, in my room at Beth's, I struggle with sleep, imagining this poor dog alone in such miserable and desolate conditions. It's almost winter, and he has no shelter, not even a blanket to keep warm.

The next morning, we walk straight to the kennel to check on him. He's gone! A town worker tells us that our homeless lab found the strength overnight to bend the chain-link wire and escape from his prison. My heart sings with joy. Run free, little one, and find yourself a home!

At first glance, Eldon is a typical sleepy place, with a population of 967 in just over one square mile. The main street is only a couple of blocks long. So why does Eldon speak to me so much that I stay a week?

The simplicity of living in a small country town is restorative and good for the soul.

While walking Yoda past some grain bins, I enjoy an impromptu lesson in soybean harvesting from two friendly men who make their living storing and then transporting the crop.

Beth and I both remember the delicious aromas of crockpot dinners simmering all day long in our Midwest childhood homes, so we make a couple of tasty slow cooker meals ourselves that would make our mothers proud.

I love our morning walks through the shimmering frost-covered soybean fields. I'd engage in some serious outdoor lounging if it weren't so cold. With one of Beth's lattes in hand,

I could gaze for hours at the beautiful frost crystals forming a light, sparkly layer over the grass fields. Nature's art gives Grant Wood a serious run for his money. So many little pleasures here have nothing to do with money, status, or Oscar nominations, like watching orange-breasted robins, crimson cardinals, and the red-headed woodpeckers everywhere in the Midwest this time of year.

The people of Eldon are authentic, honest, friendly, and genuinely nice. Eldon is the type of town where Bill, the sheriff, hands out Charms Blow Pops (yes, even to the adults); Shirley, the mayor, will stop by for coffee; Molly from the Visitors' Center will bring you homemade yogurt for breakfast; and a local phone tree results in a group of townspeople spontaneously getting together to make homemade horseradish on a Sunday afternoon.

One of my favorite Eldon social activities is the night when I assist Jim, the older man who calls out numbers for the weekly bingo game. Yes, bingo. It happens at the community center, where many silver-haired players bring plastic food storage bags of Lucky Charms mixed with peanuts and M&M's. They share their snacks as they drink hot tea and cider out of paper coffee cups. Jim and I sit in front of the room at a folding table, with a framed poster of *American Gothic* behind us. A woman cries out "Bingo!" When Beth rushes to the woman's table to collect the bingo card, her eyes twinkle. She seems more relaxed and content than she has since her husband died.

She brings the card over for us to double-check the winning numbers, pauses for a moment with a smile, and says, "You look as though you're having fun."

"Thanks, Beth. I am. Bingo is fun!" *I never imagined bingo giving me an infusion of happiness.*

For the most part, my time in the American Gothic House is quiet; my worries about the future begin to subside in a poetic simplicity, and I focus entirely on the present tasks, smiling as I savor the warmth of a teacup in my hands.

Of course, a universal law is that nothing in life can be perfect. Yoda makes certain of it. Even though the American Gothic House is a tourist attraction, many people are unaware that it's a private residence. They will often wander onto the front porch and peer into the windows, which can be unsettling for even the most well-behaved dog. Tourists regularly dress in costumes of the era in the painting and show up carrying props provided by the neighboring visitors' center to recreate the *American Gothic* masterpiece. They stand in a designated spot for a photograph in front of the modest white farmhouse. Some people pose as the man in the painting, clutching a pitchfork and wearing denim overalls, a dark jacket, and round glasses. Others will dress as the woman, wearing a dark dress with a white collar and a broach at the neck, covered by a full-body brown colonial print apron.

On our last day in Eldon, a couple who look particularly menacing to Yoda (one is wearing a hat) look in the front window. Yoda runs toward them, and then (in a moment I will replay in slow motion over and over in my head for years to come), he jumps up on the window to bark at them, and the paper-thin glass of this 121-year-old historic house shatters into a hundred little pieces. Time stops. Yoda stands still in shock. I freeze in horror. The tourists slowly back away with fear in their eyes. Only Beth is unfazed by my dog's act of blatant vandalism. Thankfully, Yoda hasn't cut himself. He's just scared the crap out of me. We find a glass repair shop in the neighboring town, and it only costs fifty-three dollars to replace the window.

The next morning, I load up Princess Leia and park on the grass in front of the house. Beth and I pose for a photo with the famous white house and a U.S. flag flying full mast behind us. Our photo seems as Americana as Beth's apple pie: the road tripper meets Ms. American Pie, and the modest farmhouse symbolizes rural American values.

"I'm going to miss you. Thank you for making me unpack." I laugh as I tightly hug Beth.

She smiles and hugs me back. "Take my house rules with you on the road. They're good for the soul."

As we drive away from the American Gothic House, I blow Beth a kiss and know I'll forever be grateful to her for opening her heart and home. This stop on the road has helped me come back to life, teaching me another lesson of the road, about how important it is to stop, slow down, and appreciate the simple things in life. Duh. It's cliché, yet so true, and I know this. Sometimes, I need the reminder to hit pause and take a breath. I turn onto the rural highway with Beth's sage words still ringing: "We should eat pie all the time because pie heals, pie is comfort food, and pie makes people happy."

TWELVE
Pardeeville

We're headed to Wisconsin to see my family, with a pit stop in Bettendorf, Iowa, to visit my early childhood home and, in one of those crazy small world coincidences, Grant Wood Elementary School, which I attended through the third grade. Although hardly a museum, my elementary school had prints of Grant Wood's paintings hanging in the halls, including an *American Gothic* poster. It's bizarre that I have just spent over a week living in the house featured in a painting that made such an impression on me in grade school.

Driving through Iowa farmland, I'm pretty chill. Calm. Warm and fuzzy. It isn't quite Zen nirvana, and it certainly isn't clarity about my life, but it's something. Something good. The simple country life has set something in motion internally, yet I can't quite describe it. A subtle shift of sorts. My drive to Bettendorf is short, taking only about three hours. I'm grateful to have recently reconnected with Heidi, my childhood friend from Salt Lake City, and she has arranged for me to spend the night at her mom's house. I have a couple of hours until her mom is home from work at 5:30 p.m., so I drive straight to Sycamore Terrace to visit the house my family lived in for four years.

Walking Yoda up and down the street fills me with childhood memories of playing with my sisters and Heidi. We stop in front of our old home. I try to reconcile my memory of it as a palatial structure with the reality of the little house before me.

I'm shaken out of my reverie by two skinny tween boys beginning a fistfight in the front yard of a house a couple of doors away. Their nylon backpacks lie on the ground at their feet, and one yells, "You're a loser!" as he throws an air punch, too far away to make contact. The other boy jumps back with his fists clenched near his face as his prepubescent voice betrays him and cracks when he bellows, "No, you're a loser!"

I march right over and ask them exactly what they expect to accomplish by hurting each other. Their eyes widen as they stop and stare at Yoda and me. I tell them to go home and never fight again. Without saying a word, they grab their backpacks, turn, and run away in opposite directions. I hope I'm teaching them a lesson; instead, they likely think I'm a crazy old lady, and they'll probably pick up the fight tomorrow.

Unfortunately, such lessons often don't stick until people experience for themselves how crappy it feels to hurt another person. Maybe that's what's happening with me now on my road trip. Perhaps I need to experience these lessons of the road to find shama. I can read about other people's experiences and how they learned from them, how they went through hell and came out enlightened and all, but there's nothing like experiencing the dark abyss for myself and then clawing my way back to the light. I must live it to learn it.

Yoda and I walk around the corner to see Grant Wood Elementary School. I expect to be stirred with emotion by the sight of my first school, but it doesn't look familiar to me with the extensive remodeling. However, walking around to the back and the steep, sloping hill where we spent our recesses does move me. I remember giggling into hands cupped around my mouth while a little blond friend wearing a fuzzy blue jacket preached emphatically that all boys had germs. I can picture rolling down the hill in warm weather with Heidi, leaving green grass stains on our pants. In the winter, we'd sled down that same snow-covered hill, snowflakes sticking to our lashes as the wind whipped our cheeks bright red, with an exhilarated sense of freedom as we picked up speed and flew free without a care in the world. Those are the childhood experiences I wish I could bottle up and take a swig of when necessary to temper the mundane world of adulting.

Heidi's mom brings takeout fish fry home for dinner, and we spend a quiet evening in her restored Victorian house, talking about Heidi's and my childhood antics and her dreams for the future now that she is recently divorced from Heidi's father. Getting to know her as an adult after not seeing her for almost twenty years is a lovely gift.

The next morning, I leave early to drive to my parents' house because I've promised them I'll be there in time for lunch. We pass resting winter farmland with landscapes the color of smoked glass, then undulating hills, rocky cliffs, sprawling plains, idyllic lakes, and dense woods. My roots are in Wisconsin, so my DNA makes me appreciate the beauty all the more. It's the blandest time of year, to boot. The colorful autumn leaves have already dropped, leaving the trees bare; the cornfields are harvested and cleared for the season. Yet I still look around with wonder. The red barns and silver silos make me smile. For raw beauty, Wisconsin farmland is as picturesque as the ocean cliffs Yoda and I visited in Big Sur.

About a mile from my parents' house, I round a curve on the two-lane rural highway and see hundreds of sandhill cranes in a cornfield. Only a couple of weeks ago, Yoda and I traveled to North

Platte to see the cranes during their winter migration south and didn't spot one. Yet now, without searching for them and practically in my parents' backyard, I see an entire field of them.

Isn't that true in life? The more desperately I chase after something, the more elusive it seems. I think of Harry.

Pulling over, I climb out of the car to watch the cranes. Yoda stays in the car, alert and watching through the window. The cranes greet me with their prehistoric trilling trumpet call. It's as if the clouds part and the angels look down and sing "Hallelujah, welcome home!"

The closer I get to my parents' house, the bigger the knot in my throat grows. When I pull into the driveway, and my mom and dad open the front door with their arms ready for hugs, the floodgates burst and I start to cry. Although I visit a few times every year, I never dreamed Princess would be in Wisconsin, that Yoda would ever spend time at my parents' house, or that I would be on a road trip for these reasons. Yet here I stand in my parents' foyer. After I've unleashed Yoda, he runs around exploring the house, sniffing every inch to gather as much information as he can.

"Oh, is it ever good to see you," Mom says. "Are you thirsty? I'll get you a drink of water." She heads to the kitchen.

Dad squeezes my shoulder. "You stay put, and I'll unload the car. I've got this."

"Thanks, Dad. But no need, I'll pull out what I need in a bit."

"Well then, I'll give my granddog some love," he says as he crouches down in the living room and playfully tussles with Yoda.

Alone in the foyer, I look out the picture window and see a great blue heron standing at the end of the pier on the lake they live on. It has an elongated, graceful S-shaped neck, and its blue-grey plumage rustles in the wind. Standing stock-still on long, thin legs, it patiently waits for a fish to swim by. I understand why Wisconsin's Menominee Tribe has a Great Blue Heron Clan. In Native American folklore, this majestic bird symbolizes patience and wisdom. If I'm patient with the lessons I'm learning on this road trip, I'll eventually tap into the wisdom I need to find shama.

Being here right now is something I'm trying to wrap my head around. I've lived 2,000 miles from my family for the past fifteen years. That means there are many mundane things in our lives that we don't share that other families do. For many people, things that feel commonplace—like having my car parked in their driveway or my dog in their living room—feel extraordinary to me. By choosing to build a life in California, I've missed out on so much: family birthday parties; my nieces' and nephews' swim meets, soccer games, and school plays; lazy weekend nights with my sisters, eating popcorn and drinking red wine while we watch a movie together.

Although I grew up in a suburb of the capital city of Madison, my parents have lived in a village named Pardeeville for the past four years. As teenagers, my sisters and I made fun of the place, even though we had never visited. How could you not ridicule a location with such a name, especially when the village has a population of less than 2,000 with many Amish farms surrounding it? Pardeeville may not be "party-ville," yet it is paradise. My parents built their house on a quiet lake. In the summer, we swim, kayak, enjoy cocktails on the pontoon boat, and marvel at the herons, ospreys, turtles, and wild mink that live around the lake.

In the winter, the lake offers different delights. Every morning during the ten days that I am here, I have coffee on the sun porch in front of a fire, at times watching bald eagles plunge into the water to grab a fish. Flocks of geese constantly squawk as they fly overhead. The lake freezes over, is blanketed with the first heavy snowfall of the season, thaws, and freezes again. My simple country life experience at the American Gothic House is continuing here at my parents' home.

One morning, after walking Yoda, I sit on the bank of the lake. The frozen water is like mirrored glass, reflecting the pillowy clouds in the sky. I focus on the space between breaths—that sacred emptiness from which all of life is created. It's a realm of profound peace and vibrant awareness. This. This is shama. Then, as soon as I recognize the moment for what it is, it slips through my fingers and sails away like a morning fog dancing over the ice. Taunting me. Now you see me, now you don't.

Today is Thanksgiving. The air is filled with a heady bouquet of pumpkin and apple pies cooling on the counter, cranberry sauce bubbling on the stovetop, and turkey with stuffing, which has been roasting in the oven since the crack of dawn. It's the smell of gratitude—the aroma of love. One of the things in life for which I'm most thankful is my family. My three sisters and I have a nickname we use when referring to one another. It started as a joke. When I first moved to LA, in a weak moment of homesickness, I wrote a sappy email telling them they were so special to me that I see stars when I think of them. As a result, I told them I would call them my seestars instead of sisters. They latched onto the concept and ran with it, and now, one private joke and fifteen years later, it's still what we call each other.

I have been counting the days to this holiday because we can rarely gather everyone together. The twins, Deb and Didi, are ER nurses, so they often work holidays. That, combined with me only making it home two or three times a year, makes it challenging to pull off large family gatherings. My seestars all married and had children, so now I have seven adorable nieces and nephews. My sister Betsy is hosting Thanksgiving at her home this year, and some of Betsy's and Didi's extended family members are joining us. That makes a whopping twenty-two people at the dinner table. The vibe is very Norman Rockwell.

I see happiness in the bright eyes and sparkling smiles of everyone in the room. They all have healthy, loving families, beautiful homes, and jobs that they enjoy. Even though no one's life can ever be truly perfect, my parents and my sisters are, at least on this day, truly content with theirs.

I've lived a very different life, including moving across the country when everyone else stayed close to home. I thought I was moving away to find my fairy-tale future, yet here we are at the Thanksgiving table, with my seestars surrounded by their kids and spouses, and I'm alone with my dog. It makes me miss Harry. He was always at my side during holidays, seamlessly fitting in with the dynamics of my family. I gave up my dreams of a house, a husband, and kids when Harry and I gave up on each other. Now, I'm single, child-free, unemployed, and, for the moment, living out of my car.

While everyone visits and clears the table before serving dessert, I escape to the laundry room, lean over the washing machine, and bury my head in my arms. It's not as if I'm a big slobbery sobber, but sometimes I need a private cleansing weep. The fresh scent of the box of laundry detergent beside me makes me think of a home, a family, a husband, and children. Of Harry. An audible sob catches in my throat. Why did he email and say he wants to see me? Why the hell is this situation so complicated?

I whisper through tears, "Harry, you promised. You promised."

He did promise. Twice. The night before I moved out, Harry asked if we could take a short drive up the coast to talk. Our short drive turned into a long one, and we ended up in Carpinteria, a beach town just south of Santa Barbara. It was late, so we found a hotel and stayed the night. While making love, my tears spilled over onto his face. I didn't want us to end; I wanted him to love me and commit to me. He knew I felt that way and said, "This time won't be the last. I promise. I promise."

So yeah, he did promise twice. Yet it was still the last time. I wipe my cheeks dry and rub my red-tipped nose with the back of my hand. No sense crying when I can be out there with my family eating pumpkin pie instead of staring at laundry soap.

The holidays are the tipping point of my emotions that have been precariously balanced on the edge of the precipice. Thanksgiving, Christmas, Hanukkah, New Year's Eve, Valentine's Day, and birthdays are always a time of assessment. *Where am I now? What have I done? Where am I going? Am I okay?* Holidays are like mile markers. I'm fine with Easter, Groundhog Day, and National Rescue Dog Day. But these other holidays? They undo me.

As I spend time with my nieces and nephews over Thanksgiving, marveling at how much they've grown since the last time I saw them, I consider how, as I'm near the end of my childbearing years, I'm not a mother. Unlike many women I know, I've never been able to say that I would move mountains to have my own children. When asked whether I want children, my answer has always been, "Yes, but not now."

Why have I always qualified my "yes" answer with "not now"? Maybe my lifelong uncertainty means I haven't been willing to make the sacrifices necessary to be a mom. I have always put finding the right partner ahead of being a mother, and since I haven't found the right partner, has that given me a convenient excuse for why I don't have kids? Did I say I wanted children because I thought I was supposed to want them, and maybe in saying it, subconsciously hoping it would make me want them? I adore my nieces and nephews. Possibly, being a loving aunt is my role. That's okay.

If I remove wanting children from the equation, would I yearn for Harry as much as I have been? Does the memory of Harry represent my one real shot at having a family of my own? If I admit that I don't want kids, would having Harry back in my life make me whole? I'm giving myself a headache. Soul searching is hard work.

Even though I don't tell my family these thoughts, when I sit down with my parents and Betsy for coffee the next day, Betsy says, "Kee Kee, it's been so great to see you. I'm happy that with your recent travels, you were able to join us for Thanksgiving."

"Thanks, Betsy, I'm glad, too. Even before everything blew up in LA, I've been dissatisfied with my life. I hope my road trip will bring positive change."

"We're here for you, seestar," Betsy says, while my mom and dad nod their heads, watching me with love shining through their kind eyes.

Mom says, "If your worst fear materializes and you never find inner peace, and instead run out of money from driving around the country with paper maps searching for the elusive shama, you are welcome to move in with us."

"Any of us, she means, Kee Kee. We won't abandon you, ever," says Betsy.

"That's so good to know, you guys. Thank you."

When the season's first major snowstorm hits while I'm in Wisconsin, I borrow my mom's winter boots, grab the leash, and take Yoda outside for a walk. The branches of smaller frostbitten trees are beginning to sag under the growing blanket of heavy, wet flakes. The snow rises to meet my feet, reminding me how I love the crunching underfoot. I can't say Yoda feels the same about walking on ice with his pampered paws, but I laugh when he sneezes as flakes land on his nose. I can only imagine how confused my Southern California boy is about this white, wet, cold stuff falling from the sky.

The last day that I'm in Wisconsin, my parents, Yoda, and I visit Amish farms around the Pardeeville area. Driving down the country roads, we're met by Amish buggies clopping along. The Amish smile and wave at us and everyone else who passes by. Has their simple way of life brought them shama? We go to the Amish bakery, the Amish cheese maker, the Amish furniture builder, the Amish general store, and best of all, the Amish candy maker who makes the best chocolate-covered toffee I've ever tasted—a sublime crisp, caramelized confection that melts in my mouth. I think her secret is adding butter. Lots of it. Perhaps that is also the secret to finding contentment in life. I should take my life, no matter what state it's in, and figuratively slather butter all over it. Nothing is ever perfect, because perfection doesn't exist. However, if I thickly spread on the butter, a life that once seemed empty or meaningless might begin to taste more delicious.

Butter makes everything better. The butter in my life is my family. It's quite fitting that my home, the Dairy State, delivers this latest lesson of the road. For that, this week after Thanksgiving, I am truly thankful.

THIRTEEN

Milwaukee and Chicago

Yoda perks up as we drive by a flock of twenty or so turkeys in the cornfield beside the interstate. They walk single file through the spotty ground fog, periodically scratching the dirt as they forage for food. Instead of celebrating their freedom, they are oblivious to the good fortune that they didn't end up on anyone's Thanksgiving dinner table.

We're en route to Chicago, with a short detour in Milwaukee to visit my friend Cendra, a woman with cerebral palsy and a developmental disability who has been in my life for nineteen years. She's a tall, overweight black woman with an unstable gait and a heart of gold.

Growing up, I was passionate about volunteering with people with developmental disabilities, because each interaction brought great moments of personal reward and growth. I was committed to pursuing a career where I could make a difference in the world. How have I gotten so off track with what matters in life? People matter, and making a difference matters. Movie sets, red carpet parties, impressive job titles, and fancy cars mean nothing in the grand scope of life. Those things all too often left me feeling alone. I feel alive with that wonderful feeling of connecting with another human when volunteering with programs like Best Buddies. That organization provides opportunities for friendships with people with intellectual and developmental disabilities.

Cendra and I met through Best Buddies and have kept in touch over the years through phone calls and letters. She writes poems for me and sends drawings of the two of us holding hands. I send her gifts from the lengthy wish lists she sends me. She doesn't have many people to give her the simple things that she wants, like makeup, perfume, a boom box, costume jewelry, bath products, and, more importantly, intangible things such as friendship and love. I haven't seen Cendra in over ten years, so after cracking the windows and leaving Yoda in the car, I eagerly ring the doorbell to her group home.

She quickly opens the door, but before she throws herself into my arms, she puts her hands on her hips, looks me up and down and says, "Girl, you have so many wrinkles!"

Having a friend like Cendra is like giving myself a shot of truth serum. My time with her always opens my heart. She's honest, vulnerable, and full of love. Cendra grabs my hand and takes me to her room. As we pass the hallway mirror, I fight the urge to sneak a peek at my reflection to assess exactly how many wrinkles I have.

Cendra sits me down on her bed and then proceeds to conduct a show-and-tell of her belongings. She hands me a weathered teddy bear.

"I've named her Kee Kee after you."

She pushes the oversized plastic glass frames higher on the bridge of her nose and then opens a jewelry box I sent her seven or eight years ago.

"Can you fix this?" She holds up the necklace I made for her long ago as a gift. The linked chain has broken.

"Sure, honey. I'll take it with me and mail it back to you once it's as good as new." So I don't lose it, I tuck the necklace into my change purse amongst the nickels and dimes. I'm glad I have my jewelry-making supplies with me. It should be an easy fix.

Cendra sits on the bed next to me and starts telling me about a guy she likes, whom she sees occasionally at events organized by the Southeastern Wisconsin branch of United Cerebral Palsy. She's animated and giggling as she talks about him.

Some of my most important teachers in life have come in unexpected forms. Over the years, Cendra has taught me about patience, the power of being non-judgmental, and the great rewards of opening my heart and life to someone less fortunate than me.

I feel a lingering sadness when I leave Cendra. Even though I've not found a way to advance the rights of persons with developmental disabilities through my work, maybe a career in this field isn't the only way to make a difference. I've encountered many forks in the road where I decided to follow inspiration or reject it out of fear of the unknown. Pursuing a career in the film industry instead of choosing a profession where I'm actively helping others was a choice that created a movement of energy in that direction. While it's tempting to second-guess my choice, is there ever a wrong choice? Maybe everything we do is part of a grand master plan of the Divine, meaning there is always good that comes from every choice we make.

So, just as I've made a difference in Cendra's life, she's enriched mine. Even simple things, like when Cendra, filled with excitement and hope, talked about the new guy she's already calling her boyfriend, inspires me with excitement and hope for what's ahead of me on the road. Or that broken necklace in my wallet—repairing it is a good reminder to look in the mirror— not to find wrinkles, but to take stock of what needs fixing in my life. These modest little interactions are potentially hugely transformative to the people involved.

Collectively, when people uplift even one other person, these interactions significantly impact the world. That's because they have a snowball effect: When I do something nice for someone, they are apt to pay it forward by doing something nice for someone else. Even while trying to make an impression on the bigger community of humanity through my career choice, I am still one of the many little snowflakes in that growing snowball. My friendship with Cendra is as valuable as making a blockbuster film in the grand scheme of things, because we make a difference in each other's lives.

I've been thinking a lot about fear while I drive. It's similar to how fire needs fuel, oxygen, and heat. We aren't born afraid; we're born open and eager to explore the world. However, as we age, we begin to seek security and safety. We stop taking risks and keep a low profile. For instance, when my unique ideas are mocked, ridiculed, or shot down—in a job, a relationship, or even in the classroom early in life—the judgment stings. So, the next time around, we sidestep getting the metaphorical crap kicked out of us. Whenever we aren't true to ourselves, to avoid judgment or failure, we effectively flick another spark onto a pile of discarded dreams. Soon, the sparks catch, we hear a crackle, and the fire of fear ignites. The small fires and sparks were there all along, but letting the pile grow can lead to third-degree burns when the bonfire catches.

I've often lived with a blazing fear of failure and of being judged, alone, and unaccepted—and of driving at night. Along with that fun stuff, I had questions: Why did I want to leave Wisconsin? Why did I feel I didn't fit in? Why did I choose differently than my peers? I wanted to go to New York, Los Angeles, and Chicago and explore the rest of the world. In my twenties, I couldn't envision getting married, buying a house, or having kids. My priority was always to seek out the meaning of life. Sometimes, I thought there was something wrong with me.

My torment increased when I imagined I might hurt my loved ones by giving them the impression that I rejected their way of life. I worried that they might take my choices personally. So, rather than risk hurting my family, I've stayed in a painful place of limbo, neither completely living my life, nor living the life I thought they expected me to lead. It's all about fear.

Yet here's what I'm now learning: I imagined I was an outcast in my family and society, when I have always completely belonged. My visit home this time helped me see things differently. My family has never judged me in life, even though at times, when they would question some of my choices, I felt I was disappointing them. Now it's clear that their questions were more about trying to understand, not ridicule. Strangely, my fear of being judged kept me from seeing that my family has always been proud of me, quirks and all. So, all that fear was me overthinking and overreacting as usual. I would imagine someone having conversations about me in their head, thinking they were criticizing. It's evident to me now that I'm the only person who has judged me. I alone created the restrictive boundaries within which I have lived. I've built my own walls. I've done it to myself.

Most of my life choices have been the safe option. I've clung to my rule-following, conformist, oxygen-sapping decisions as necessary for my security. Can I want too much security in life? I'm not sure security truly exists; instead, it's an illusion. I've been afraid of losing some of that perceived security, so I've clung to my daily routine, and then, after years of attempting to break the glass ceiling with a career I didn't want, I was laid off. Now I see that I need to take more risks and figure out my own rules, stop fanning the remaining glowing embers of that fire of fear, and reclaim my oxygen.

Have no regrets. What about going to law school? Other than a mountain of student loan debt, it gave me some great friends. But living across the country and working long hours hasn't made it easy to keep in touch. I haven't seen most of them in nearly sixteen years. Wanting to close that gap, Yoda and I leave Milwaukee and head to Chicago for the night to reconnect with a few of my friends from that long-ago chapter.

The evening weather in Chicago is too cold to leave Yoda in the car. Because of his separation anxiety, I can't leave him alone in the hotel room. So, instead of piling into one of our old watering holes, I invite everyone over to my hotel—a musty room on a dusty floor undergoing renovation. Not the Ritz.

Five friends who can break free of work and family obligations come to my hotel room for fried chicken, beer, and tequila—finally, I won't drink tequila alone.

They've all become highly successful. One is a gold-medal-winning and world-record-holding Paralympic athlete, public speaker, and disability lawyer. I'm equally impressed by the others—their careers include a senior executive with an international hotel chain, two who own businesses, and another with a part-time practice. That last one also raises energetic twins who are jumping up and down on one of the beds. I'm in awe of my friends and all they have achieved. I'm embarrassed to be the only one in the group without a job. It's human nature to compare oneself with others, but I should know better.

My longtime friends sprawl on the two queen beds, and Yoda jumps from one bed to the other, relishing in the endless belly rubs. Our laughter and conversation turn into a stroll down memory lane. Law school was intense, challenging, and a helluva lot of work. We were all broke, so even if we had the time to go out, we couldn't afford much of anything, making our relationships more important and rewarding. Together, we studied, struggled, laughed, and shared lockers.

Over the years, my memory of law school has been selective—thinking about the pain and not remembering the good times. I had a lot of fun with my friends and studies. Do I wish I didn't have the student debt load that I carry? Hell yeah. Do I wish that I had never attended law school? No. My education and law school friendships helped make me who I am today: an aimless traveler. Well, I'm not exactly aimless—I'm seeking shama, and hoping my circumstances are temporary. The whole law school experience is now a part of me, and it's helped shape me in many ways. It's a revelation that by stepping back from the repetitious daily anxiety of my unfulfilling Hollywood life (and thus not stoking that smoldering fire of fear), I kinda like who I am at the core.

So dammit, have no regrets.

Being in the kind of flux I've been in, it's easy to get down on myself about this or that path taken in life. I should have done this; I shouldn't have done that. Yet once I step back and reflect on where each perceived "bad" choice has taken me, it's clear why I had to make that choice. In addition to spending years regretting law school, I've often regretted moving to LA. Yet, if I hadn't moved to LA, I wouldn't have met many people who have influenced and touched my life in ways greater than

I could have ever imagined. If I hadn't moved to LA, I might not have discovered my spiritual path or my love for health and wellness (and yoga pants).

So, back to my choice to take a job making movies over doing something more meaningful. Well, I don't regret that either. Making movies was a dream of mine from a young age. If I hadn't worked in the film industry, I'd venture a guess that I'd be working in a different field, wondering "What if I had pursued my dream of working in Hollywood?"

Have no regrets.

To label choices "right" or "wrong" isn't helpful. I have no option but to own my choices; whether consciously or not, I made them for a reason. I have faith that, one day, it will all make sense. It's so easy to get lost in the "What if?" and "Why didn't I?" I gotta give that up.

The hard lesson of the road that I'm trying to learn: Have no regrets.

FOURTEEN
St. Louis and Branson

Yoda and I leave Chicago on Route 66 and drive through Missouri almost entirely on what John Steinbeck famously nicknamed The Mother Road. This stretch is a timeless road trip.

Route 66 was one of the first U.S. highways, originally running from Chicago to Los Angeles. My apartment in Santa Monica is close to the western finish of Old Route 66. There's even a Route 66 "End of the Trail" sign at the Santa Monica Pier, marking the official end of the *Main Street of America*. Driving Route 66 embodies the spirit of Americana. It is a trip back in time, with plenty of rural retro kitsch. I know people obsessed with the history and lore (or is it lure?) of Route 66, many of whom have taken road trips on segments of the Old Route. It seems to carry with it a certain romantic nostalgia. I've never given it much thought. Now, I get it. The classic, white-lettered Route 66 shield painted on the highway's black asphalt, over-the-top, fun neon signage, 1950s retro motels, vintage diners, soda fountains, larger-than-life fiberglass statues, and mom-and-pop stores along the road make me smile.

Instead of playing my sappy, soul-searching, sad road trip playlist, I turn my iPod on shuffle and skip any song that isn't light and playful. Brooding over life is tiresome, and I need a break. Up until now, my road trip lessons have been heavy. Often wracked with emotion, I've been intentionally letting myself feel my pain. I've been wrapping myself up in my angst and owning it the only way I know how: submerging myself in it and then going to battle. I must do the work to grow. By not putting a bandage on it, I'm finally dealing with my crap once and for all. Line 'em up, knock 'em down.

I've been hauling an emotional load on the road, but here on Route 66, my outlook is light. As a feather. The sun is shining, the air crisp, the sky clear, and I can't wipe the lopsided grin off my face.

While driving, I chatter away to Yoda and Princess.

"I am beginning to think I might come out on top at the end of the day. Remember when we first hit the road, I had a premonition that instead of running away from my life, I may be running toward my future? Well, that feels more real than ever," I say to my two road trip comrades. They're good listeners. "You guys, the *lessons of the road* are so meaningful to me."

Each place we visit teaches me a profound lesson about how to go about life. I proceed to list everything I'm learning—from how the Pismo Beach monarchs demonstrated that change doesn't happen overnight, to how the chickens in Salt Lake City taught me to take control of my life by facing fears, to my epiphany in a remote hotel room in Cheyenne that I'm not alone. The big test will be when this trip is over, I must continuously *live* the things I'm learning. Every spiritual teaching I've ever received has said there's never a permanent arrival at some total nirvana-like state of mind.

"We are all always works in progress. Right, Yoda?"

Yoda lets out a lazy groan as he stretches and shifts position on his bed in the back of the car. It's almost as if he is rolling his eyes and saying, "Okay, Ma, whatever you say. I'm going back to sleep now."

I laugh out loud. Have I doggone lost it? Because, well, I am anthropomorphizing my dog and my car. They've become my travel companions and confidantes. They've seen more raw emotion in me than I've ever let any human see, and they haven't abandoned me. Will the same go for my friends and colleagues? Can I possibly be honest, vulnerable, and real without scaring the crap out of them? There is no turning back; I'm jumping in.

The road, she's a special one. Leading me to shama. Straight ahead, twists and turns, and don't run out of gas.

I pull into a rest stop in Conway, Missouri, with a Route 66 theme, including a flashing 1950s-inspired *Route 66 Welcome to Missouri* neon sign. The picnic shelters, designed as mini pavilions, resemble a diner, market, barbershop, motel, filling station, and other businesses seen along Old Route 66. In the restroom, I almost whoop out loud when I spot the world's most functionally fantastic public restroom sink. This automatic hand washer/dryer is a space-age-like, ridiculously awesome sink. I hold my hands in one place, and first, it automatically squirts soap into my hands. Then, it sprays warm water, and finally, it blows warm air. It's so fascinating that I wash my hands a second time. This über-cool Route 66 rest stop item is free for all to enjoy. How many other travelers are as delighted with the discovery of this George Jetson sink?

It's still daylight when we arrive in St. Louis, so, as we do when landing at each new overnight stop, Yoda and I take a long walk to stretch our stiff road trip muscles. We wander along a gravel path surrounding a pond with hundreds of geese. A group of waterfowl waddle onto the path in front of us and then square off their stance while staring me in the eye. Maybe these gregarious birds have picked up on my lighthearted mood and are playing with us? Another gaggle of geese waddles up behind us, blocking our forward and backward paths. Yoda hides behind my right leg as if to say that *I* need to protect *him*. Thanks, heroic guard dog.

"Shoo," I implore, waving my arms and stomping. These ballsy geese won't budge. Hmmm, maybe they aren't being playful after all, and instead are being territorial? Remembering that geese can be mean, I tug Yoda's leash, and we walk a long, wide circle in the grass off the path around the geese to get back to our hotel. Crisis averted.

"Welcome to St. Louis. My name is Dean. Let me know if you need anything."

Dean, in his mid-thirties, stands awkwardly behind the hotel reception desk, his khakis endearingly belted a little high on his waist. He laughs self-consciously as he brushes his wavy bangs from his eyes.

"Thank you. We're happy to be here after driving all day."

He blushes. "Can I pet your dog?"

"Sure." I can see that Dean loves dogs.

After a moment, it's clear that Dean loves Yoda.

"Would it be possible to get a fridge in my room so I can put some food from my cooler in it for the night?" I ask.

"Of course. You know, we aren't full, so how about we move you to another room that has a fridge?"

Dean helps me move to another room down one floor, carrying a couple of bags while I bring Yoda and his bed. Then, for the next few minutes, Dean lies down on my new room's floor and wrestles with Yoda. He smiles on his way out as he gives Yoda a little rub behind the ears, and says, "Bring a toy to the lobby when you take him out for his evening walk. I wanna play with him some more."

A couple of hours later, we're in the lobby again, and Yoda and Dean are back at it. On his break, Dean went out and bought Yoda some beef jerky—the good stuff. Yoda has made another friend on the road.

These simple friendly encounters are becoming my favorite parts of this road trip. Dean and Yoda tussle together on the floor of the lobby with Yoda's favorite toy (a stuffed macaw named Chico with one eye, a partially chewed-off beak, and stuffing that falls out of a hole in one of its multicolored wings). Yoda loves men. I've never been able to give him a daddy.

Dean laughs and throws Chico across the room for Yoda to chase. I can see Yoda giving Dean as much joy as Dean gives Yoda. Driving around the country attempting to create a life beyond tears, we just may be leaving a bit of happiness in our wake.

At 9 a.m., I'm already on my second cup of coffee. Once again, Route 66 (now Highway 44) doesn't disappoint. When I pass a trio of large, colorful teepees just east of Exit 242, I backtrack and make my way to what turns out to be the Indian Harvest Trading Post. It's a store in a teepee, run by a friendly Native American couple who sell merchandise made by members of between twelve and twenty tribes. I buy Yoda some buffalo jerky and myself a dream catcher to hang from Princess's rearview mirror. Dream catchers hang above a person sleeping to catch and hold the bad dreams and let the good dreams or important messages through to the dreamer. Although I don't intend to fall asleep at the wheel while driving Princess, I figure I can certainly use a boost with all the daydreaming I do during long hours on the road.

My new dream catcher hangs along with necklaces made from Job's Tears and Huayruro seeds, given to me by women from the

Shipibo Indigenous tribe when I was in the Peruvian Amazon, and prayer beads blessed by Amma, a Hindu spiritual leader known as "The Hugging Saint." On the left side of my dashboard sits a shiny purple Ganesh brought back to me from India by a yoga teacher friend and a good luck blue kyanite crystal I bought on a road trip a couple of years ago in Ukiah, California. Of course, my favorite and most important dashboard adornment is my duct-taped decade-old "I Welcome Change" sticky note. The dashboard is becoming so eclectic and filled with talismans that it seems to fit right in with the kitsch of Route 66. Even if these things won't bring me good luck or protect me from evil, at least they bring another smile to my face.

Endless signs for shows and attractions appear alongside the road for two hours before we arrive in Branson. Andy Williams has a musical variety Christmas show at the Moon River Theater, named after his song "Moon River," which is also my parents' song and first dance at their wedding. There's a billboard for the Tony Orlando and the Lennon Sisters Christmas Celebration. My grandma was a huge fan of the Lennon Sisters when they were on the Lawrence Welk Show, and she often told my sisters and me that her dream was to see us singing on the Lawrence Welk Show, too. I pass a giant sign for The Osmonds' show, with the brothers flashing their signature toothy grins. Tuning into two different Branson radio stations, my smile continues because so much of the programming is over-the-top cheesy. With the turn signal as a metronome, I drum my hands on the steering wheel and hum along with the music.

The corniness grows in the city. It seems like a mini Las Vegas for silver-haired folks. I drive the strip and take photos from the car, not once tempted to get out and walk around. I'd rather find a good hiking spot than spend our time walking amongst all that neon. Of course, I may feel different about Branson in forty years. Perhaps it will be a future road trip destination instead of simply an overnight stop. Maybe I'll venture here in my eighties to see a Lady Gaga or Pearl Jam tribute band.

I imagined my three-day trip driving through Missouri would be mostly forgettable. But I've smiled through the entire length of the state. Miles of smiles. This state has reminded me that each day can be an adventure if I let it. I am pretty certain that this same canon will apply when (or if) I settle back into life off the road. I want my light to shine, and the only way for that to happen is for me to start breaking my own rules. Then maybe, just maybe, my carefree, intuitive, individual inner child will come out to play, speak the truth, and live purely in the moment. I'd like it if she'd stay awhile.

Missouri has taught me my most recent lesson of the road: simple, lighthearted fun can be found everywhere if I keep my eyes and heart open, be in the moment, and seek out the playfulness that each day has to offer.

FIFTEEN

Hot Springs — A Park Ranger

After St. Louis, I leave Route 66 and head south through the rugged Arkansas Ozarks on Scenic Byway 7. The road winds through the mountains and past waterfalls, streams, valleys, rocky cliffs, and rivers, and I pull into scenic lookouts several times to take in the stunning vistas. The highway leads me into Hot Springs, Arkansas.

The magic is evident as soon as I drive into the historic downtown area of President Bill Clinton's boyhood hometown, nestled in the Ouachita Mountain Range. Steam from the abundant natural hot springs floats out from the street vents into the chilly, crisp December air like a light fog rolling across the road. Forty-seven springs are in Hot Springs National Park, the nation's only national park located within city limits (confusingly, this city was initially named Hot Springs National Park and is now called Hot Springs). The national park has over twenty miles of hiking trails and a few free-flowing natural springs. Three thousand years ago, Native Americans named this area "Valley of the Vapors." Today, most of the springs are capped; however, originally, all forty-seven springs bubbled up mineral-enriched 147-degree water. During those times when the springs flowed freely, the lush valley would be filled with steam every morning, making for some awe-inspiring rainbows as the sun broke through.

As usual, the first thing to do after parking the car is to walk Yoda. We stroll through the part of the national park called Arlington Lawn, which has captured the spirit of the season with holiday decorations and a field of twinkling Christmas trees and reindeer formed from strands of multicolored lights. Steaming spring water cascades down the side of a hill into two stone-walled pools.

A high-pitched yip startles me. A brown and white puppy is trying to get Yoda's attention. He's not wearing a collar and is far too skinny—with ribs poking out—yet he also has a pot belly. He comes closer and spiritedly nips at Yoda's legs as we walk. I'm not sure what to do. I don't want to leave him, but I don't know where to take him. Yoda seems intrigued with the little fella and nudges him with his nose as the puppy rolls over onto his back with his tail wagging enthusiastically. As they playfully tussle, a park ranger pulls up, climbs out of his SUV, and walks over. He has a confident yet friendly vibe.

"You look like you need help."

"Yup," I say gratefully. "Right now, I need a hero."

He laughs as he bends over and reaches for the puppy, who runs behind me. He tries again without success. Each time the park ranger reaches for him, the puppy scrambles out of his reach.

"Well, this is embarrassing. I'm not the hero I claim to be."

I laugh. "Let's make a deal. You hold my dog's leash and swear up and down that you'll find the puppy a home and not turn it over to a kill shelter, and I'll get him to come to me."

"Deal."

I sit on the ground, and the little dog immediately runs into my arms, nuzzling my neck with kisses.

"He's bloated. It looks like he might have worms," says the ranger, reaching over to gently probe the dog's distended belly.

I carry the puppy to the ranger's vehicle, where we put it in the back seat and shut the door. He hands Yoda's leash back to me.

I introduce myself as I glance at the badge on his shirt. "I'm Kee Kee, and this is Yoda. We're on a road trip and rolled into town an hour ago." I'm captivated by the friendly squint of his eyes as he smiles.

"My name is Sam Musket."

"Wait, for real? Your last name is Musket, and you carry a gun?"

"It gets better," he declares. "My dad is a gun manufacturer."

"Well, I guess you were born for this career," I tease. "Is rescuing puppies in your job description?"

"Everything is in my job description if it involves Hot Springs National Park. I only moved here three months ago, so this would be my first puppy rescue."

"Where did you move from?"

"I spent the past few years in Arizona near the Mexican border working to break up drug cartels."

"It sounds dangerous."

"Yep, and it was physically taxing too." He casually leans against his truck and crosses his arms. "It gets pretty lonely out there, and I needed a break. So, I accepted a position in Hot Springs, which is where my mother now lives."

"How do you like it here? Does it feel like home yet?"

"Other than my coworkers, I don't know anyone in the city but my mom. I've been working so much that I haven't had time to date or make friends."

My heart jumps. Sam is single. His massive, ripped arms distract me. He must spend a lot of time in the gym. I crave male companionship after spending so much time alone over the past few months.

"Well, I need to take this pup to the station and get back to my rounds." He hesitates. "Would you want to get together for a drink while you're in town?"

"Sure!" I say, hoping I don't sound too enthusiastic. *Keep it chill, Keeks.*

Unfortunately, I'm only in Hot Springs for a few days, and Sam works the entire time. His shift doesn't end until 11 p.m. Although I'm usually in bed much earlier than that, I tell him that 11 p.m. tomorrow works fine. The problem is that nothing in town is open that late. Because he's temporarily living with his mom, I propose we meet at my hotel, which is something I would never normally suggest. But I have Yoda with me, and Sam is a law enforcement officer, so it seems like a safe suggestion.

We exchange numbers, and he says he'll text me tomorrow to confirm.

With a few hours of daylight left, Yoda and I take a walk down Central Avenue, the main street in downtown Hot Springs, where festive holiday cheer decorates all the shop windows. This street is home to the architectural gem of Bathhouse Row, eight historic bathhouses built in the late 1800s. Today, only two are open to the public. I'm excited to soak but postpone using the public baths for another day. Instead, I plan to bathe in the private mineral spring bathtub in my hotel room tonight. I splurged and booked a room at the historic Arlington Hotel, which opened its doors in 1875. Everyone from Al Capone to Babe Ruth to the occasional American president has stayed there. It sits majestically in the center of town—a striking model of Spanish colonial architecture with two domed towers and holiday decorations of a royal grandeur. A golden star shines near the roofline of the hotel, and a waterfall of strands of golden lights flows down from the star to the *porte cochere* at the entrance to the building. When I enter the lobby, I see an eight-foot-tall gingerbread house covered in thousands of candies. I'm not sure how they keep kids (or grown-ups) from feasting on all those gumdrops, peppermints, and that royal icing.

Floating in the air is a scent bouquet of melted butter and popcorn, and reflexively, I salivate where I stand in front of a gourmet popcorn shop. Colorful signs on the window promote weird popcorn flavors, such as bacon and cheddar, watermelon, and baked potato. With Yoda's leash tied to a bench, I walk in and approach a short, spunky woman with strawberry blonde hair standing behind the counter. Her name tag says, "HELLO, My Name is Brenda."

"Hi there. Would you like a sample?"

"Oh yes, please."

She hands me a small white paper cup filled with dill-pickle-flavored popcorn. It's surprisingly addictive.

"Is this your first time in our shop?"

"Yes, I arrived in town a couple of hours ago. My dog and I are on a road trip." Something makes me want to open up to her. "I just lost my job, and since I'm not sure what to do next, now seems to be the perfect time to explore the country."

"Oh boy, can I relate," she says. "I was laid off from my job in Minnesota a few months ago, so I moved to Hot Springs to live with my sister. And here I am, selling popcorn for a living."

"What did you do in Minnesota?"

"I worked in healthcare information technology. I've lived all over the world with my career, but I never thought my midlife crisis would happen in Arkansas," she says sarcastically with a laugh.

"The failing economy is gifting many of us with unexpected midlife crises," I chuckle. "I guess we're trying to figure out how to get back on our feet in unconventional ways—you through popcorn and me through driving."

While Brenda continues to feed me samples, we compare stories about coming to terms with how life isn't quite turning out as planned. Hard knocks aren't something either of us envisioned at our age. We each thought that by now, we'd be married, have a couple of grown kids, and be sitting on plush retirement accounts while vacationing on exotic beaches around the world.

Our conversation is bittersweet. On the one hand, it's nice to have someone with whom I can commiserate, but on the other hand, it drives home the irony of life. Despite wanting life to offer guarantees, there are none. No siree. We planned, worked hard, and did what we were supposed to do, and as a reward, someone pulled the rug out from under us without warning. Is this what happens when people live too long playing out a role in life in which they question the casting call? Perhaps the Universe intentionally throws a wrench into our broken lives so that we can use the tool to fix what isn't working and build something new that does.

"I'd like to purchase a large kettle corn to take back to my hotel," I say. "It feels like a popcorn-and-movie-in-bed type of night."

"I have those types of nights all the time," she titters.

I promise Brenda I'll stop by again before I leave town.

The following day, I check Yoda into a doggie daycare in town right when they open at 9 a.m. and then head out to the Ron Coleman Mine for a few hours. In talking with the hotel concierge, I was excited (the understatement of the century) to learn about the abundance of crystal deposits in the nearby

Ouachita Mountains. Arkansas has some of the highest-quality quartz in the world. Ron Coleman Mining is a commercial quartz mining operation with a designated area for the public to mine for crystals. For twenty dollars, they give me a pick tool and a large bag to fill with as many crystals as I can find—the most epic sandbox on the planet.

After wrapping my scarf around my neck to protect against the chilly December wind, I squat down next to a big mound of reddish soil and rake some dirt to the side. The sun glints off a sparkly crystal the size of a pinky with perfectly faceted sides. It looks like an expertly cut gemstone crafted by a jeweler and polished to a brilliant shine, except it wasn't human-made. Mother Nature created it, and I pulled it straight from the ground. I hold it up to the sky. It is mostly clear, and the sunlight casts a rainbow through the center of it.

After a while, I take a break from digging to check out the lush, intoxicating landscape of the mountains and towering pine trees that make up this part of the Ouachita National Forest. Unlike most mountain ranges in the U.S., the Ouachita Mountains run east to west instead of north to south. A unique geological phenomenon is going on here between the mountains, crystals, and thermal waters.

As I breathe in the fresh, zesty scent of the surrounding conifers, a deep feeling settles in that everything will be okay—the sentiment I've hoped would eventually appear on this trip. These past few months on the road have divested me of everything I previously thought was important. While sitting here in the dirt, with a pile of crystals at my side and a spectacular vista in front of me, it's clear that by stripping myself of the people, work, material items, and other things in which I've clothed myself to create my identity, I can now welcome the offerings that the Universe is leaving at my feet. Finally, after about three hours of mining crystals, I'm so cold that I can no longer feel my fingers, so I head to the parking lot rinsing station to clean my bounty before I head out.

The only other people at the mine on this blustery day are a dynamic and friendly couple from Austin with an eclectic, hippie vibe. The man has dreadlocks and wears a tie-dyed thermal shirt under his puffer vest. The woman has dark wavy hair peeking out from under a well-worn knitted hat and wears mala beads around her neck.

We stand in the parking lot comparing our crystals, and they mention that last night, they attended a fire walk hosted by a shaman who lives in the area. Wait, what? A shaman and a fire walk smack dab in the middle of the Nation's Bible Belt. And I missed it.

After I pick up Yoda from doggie daycare, we walk through Arlington Lawn. The doggie daycare worker told me that Yoda initially whined and stood at the door waiting for me to return, and then, eventually, he relaxed and even briefly played with one of the other dogs. Doggie daycare is an expense I'd rather not have, but Yoda's separation anxiety leaves no other option. I envy people who can leave their dogs alone in hotel rooms.

Yoda's tail starts wagging, and he pulls on the leash, so I turn my gaze to see why. Ranger Sam is making his rounds of the park and crouches to scratch behind Yoda's ears.

"Are we still on for tonight?" I ask.

"Yes! I'll bring my computer and show you photos from when I trekked the Appalachian Trail after college."

"Cool. How much of it did you hike?"

"All two thousand, one hundred ninety miles of it. It took me six months."

Whoa. Impressive. Sam isn't my normal type. I tend to gravitate toward tall, lean, artsy-fartsy free spirits, not beefy guys wearing bulletproof vests and carrying firearms and handcuffs. Yet bizarrely, I'm attracted to him. He's manly and rugged, with a bodybuilder physique. He radiates warmth and security.

Yoda is already tugging in a different direction, anxious to continue our walk. "Well, I look forward to seeing those photos. See you tonight." I wave as Yoda pulls me away.

My cheeks flush in the mirror of my dimly lit hotel bathroom as I apply lipstick. What would it feel like to be in this brawny man's arms and for his strong hands to hold mine?

When Sam knocks on my hotel room door, I have trouble meeting his eyes as I say hello. If only he knew what fantasies I've been stirring up while I've been waiting for him. Luckily, Yoda breaks the ice by bringing Sam his stuffed macaw toy.

"Do you want to play fetch?" He throws the toy across the room, and Yoda scampers after it, bringing it back and dropping it at Sam's feet. He tosses it a few more times, until Yoda tires of the game and curls up on his bed in the corner of the room.

"I'm impressed that you travel with his bed," observes Sam.

"There's limited space in my Prius, but I've made room for it. When I crawl into the big bed, he jumps up and snuggles next to me all night."

"Smart guy," winks Sam.

As a hot flush creeps up my neck, I try to play it cool, saying, "How about you show me those photos of your Appalachian Trail trek?"

He boots up his computer, and we start looking at photos while we sit on the bed, the only place in the room where we can sit together. Our arms touch as we share his laptop screen. I shiver, and the fine hairs on my arms stand on end. With his sleeves rolled up to his elbows, I can see his ripped forearms marked with numerous tattoos. Forearms are sexy, and Sam's are next level. They suggest a man who can fix his car, shovel snow, chop wood, make me a cup of coffee, and easily carry me across the room.

I am lonely; I want this man. His eyes tell me that the feeling is mutual. He sets the computer aside in a flash, and soon, we're breathing heavily, our bodies fervently meshed together.

It's over almost before it began, and wasn't the peak transcendent moment from my earlier daydream.

"It's been a long time, and I guess my body and brain didn't communicate tonight," Sam sheepishly apologizes as he puts his clothes back on.

"After this much time alone on the road, the touch of another human is worth more than an orgasm," I say, as I hug him goodnight before he leaves.

I've had exactly one other one-night stand in my life with a guy I met at a wedding, which turned into a two-night stand and probably would have continued had he not lived on the opposite coast. This behavior, while fun, is wildly out of character for me. Tonight is extra amusing for three reasons: (1) Sam is so completely not my type (but Harry is); (2) he carries a gun and wears a bulletproof vest (see #1); and (3) I'm obviously not a one-night stand type of girl.

Sam is leaving for vacation in two days—the day after I move on—so we make plans to see each other one more time tomorrow before he leaves town. This non-one-night-stand girl is going for two with a guy who must first remove his gun holster and body armor—one of those rare times in life when I need to throw my hands in the air and say, "What the hell. Screw it. I want to fuck."

The next night, when he arrives, he brings a gift of a couple of books about park rangers, which plays to my curiosity and questions about his job. We intertwine again more tenderly, almost as if our bodies are expressing gratitude to the other for the much-needed physical connection.

My brief experience here has been magical, and I want more. Each day, Yoda and I have gone for long hikes on Hot Springs Mountain, which is part of the Ouachita Mountain Range. I plan to get in one more long hike before we climb back into Princess tomorrow morning to spend hours on the road to wherever our next destination might be. Maybe Memphis? I'll decide tonight. For now, I still haven't soaked in the public baths.

So, after our hike, I drop Yoda off at doggie daycare and drive back to Central Avenue for a quick coffee before I head to the baths. The couple I met at the crystal mine suggested I swing by a coffee shop in town to strike up a conversation with the eccentric owner, Juan. Although they warned me that he's extreme in his metaphysical theories, they promised our discussion is bound to be colorful and filled with nuggets about the history of Hot Springs.

True to their word, Juan is passionate about his *totally out-there* spiritual beliefs. I find him amusing as I drink my soy latte, especially when he tries to convince me that aliens walk amongst us and members of the Illuminati are trying to infiltrate Hot Springs. It turns out that Juan also attended the same fire walk with the shaman that the hippies mentioned. Oh, how I wish I had arrived in town earlier to meet this shaman. He may have had some answers for me on how to find shama.

When I finish my coffee, I head over to Buckstaff Bathhouse. It's the oldest bathing facility here, operating continuously since 1912. Twenty-five dollars gives me a traditional bath, which involves being scrubbed with a loofah mitt by a personal attendant while soaking naked in a private whirlpool mineral spring bath, followed by a sitz bath, a sit in a metal vapor cabinet (that looks like a mini torture chamber), relaxing while wrapped in hot, wet towels, and then finishing with cooling off in a vintage ribcage needle shower.

An hour later, I'm contentedly sitting on a sofa in the lobby, contemplating a nap. However, I'm leaving in the morning, so now is the time for me to experience the only other working bathhouse in town. Barely dry from my first bath, I head to Quapaw Bathhouse, throw on my bathing suit, and make a beeline for the hottest of four communal thermal pools.

Once in the water, my eyes relax and close as I slide down so a water jet hits a tender spot between my shoulder blades.

There's a loud voice in my ear. "You're using my jet."

My eyes snap open to see a tall, lanky man with a mustache and silver hair, affably grinning as he sits on the edge and dangles his legs in the water beside me.

"Oh, I'm sorry. Wait, really?"

"I'm teasing you. But it is my favorite jet." He has a lazy Texas drawl.

"Well, in that case, I'll make sure that you're next in line when I give up the jet."

He slips into the water and introduces himself. "My name is Art, and contrary to popular opinion, I'm not territorial when it comes to my soaks."

As I reply, "That's good to know, Art. I'm Kee Kee," a willowy woman appears, joins us in the water, and says hello.

Art introduces us. "Kee Kee, meet Melissa, who came to Hot Springs for our recent fire walk. She's a New York artist, yoga instructor, and author who spent five years traveling around the world with U.G. Krishnamurti, the late Indian sage."

"Melissa, it's a pleasure. You must have so many stories about your travels," I exclaim.

We continue to talk, and in a twist of road trip serendipity, Art is the shaman who hosted the fire walk the other night.

Shut the front door!

"Art, I can't believe you're the shaman I've been hearing about this week. I thought I'd missed the opportunity to meet you!"

"It seems it's our destiny to meet, after all." Art smiles.

"How did you become a shaman?" I ask.

"I spent seventeen years studying under the great Lakota Medicine Man, Red Eagle. Did you know that the crystals and thermal waters are why Hot Springs, Arkansas, was originally a sacred gathering place for Indian tribes from around the country?"

"I've heard that they often designate hot springs around the country as neutral grounds to be shared in peace by all tribes."

"That's true. Healers and metaphysicists from near and far come here for the same reasons as all those ancient Indian tribes. We've got crystals, hot springs, and hiking trails to seven energy vortexes."

"One for each chakra?" I'm semi-joking.

"That's right," Art answers with a knowing smile.

Chakras are spinning energy centers in our bodies that affect our physical and emotional health. I'm pretty sure mine are out of alignment. I mean, *helloooo*, I'm the crazy girl driving around the country with my dog, trying to find inner peace.

Melissa quietly listens, eyes closed, as she relaxes in the water.

We all sit in silence for a few minutes, absorbing the restorative powers of the water.

My eyelids are heavy. *Maybe it's time to surrender the coveted jet.*

"You and my wife need to meet each other," says Art.

"Who is your wife?"

"Her name is Starr."

SIXTEEN

Hot Springs — A Curandera

Art tells me Starr is a revered seventy-two-year-old curandera, master healer, and intuitive. "She has spent decades studying with shamans, healers, curanderos, and masters in thirteen countries. Now she dedicates her life to helping others grow with their paths and destinies."

Okay, he has my full attention.

"What is a curandera?" I ask.

"A curandera is a traditional native healer, or a medicine woman. Curandero is the male version of the word." He pauses to let this information sink in, and then continues. "We live in a geodesic dome built on a hill that everyone calls 'The Dome.' Why don't you stop by tomorrow?"

I immediately accept Art's invitation, while mentally calculating how much it will cost me to book another night at The Arlington Hotel. I only budgeted for staying in Hot Springs for three nights, while, once again, this road trip reminds me it has a mind of its own.

Doggie daycare is closed, so I must take Yoda to The Dome. I scatter some treats in the car for Yoda, crack the windows so he will get some air (it's a chilly December day, so I'm not leaving him in a hot car), and then walk to the front door and knock. Art answers with a hospitable smile and walks me through the foyer straight into the front room.

A beautiful arched glass window beyond the pews and an altar overlooks a lush green landscape.

"The Dome used to be a church. Starr and I moved in many years ago, making it our home, and named the building The Divine Intervention Dome," Art explains. "Now we host gatherings on Sunday mornings in this room."

"I have a feeling your gatherings are different from the Lutheran church services of my youth."

"Well, we do call the Sunday services church, but they are different from a Protestant church service," he clarifies. "Our Sunday gatherings involve singing, guided meditation, and healings."

Cool.

"Art!" a woman's high-pitched, nasal, squawky voice yells from the other room. "Is Kee Kee here?"

In walks a rotund woman with twinkling eyes, chunky turquoise jewelry, and an impish smile. Instantly I like her, even though her commanding presence intimidates me.

Starr opens her arms for a hug, redirecting me as I'm starting to embrace her. "Left cheek to left cheek," she instructs. "Many Indigenous people believe we should hug this direction for our hearts to connect."

She slowly breathes in through her nose while giving me a long, warm hug, and I shiver with the sense that she's inhaling to experience my aura, to learn what's behind my physical exterior and who I am at the core of my being. *Oh, God. Is she seeing through my smile to the mess of a woman inside? Well then, maybe she can help.*

"Come into my office, dear. I want you to meet two former students of mine who are visiting. They are both master healers."

She leads me down the hall into her office and directs me to sit in a rolling office chair as the two women introduce themselves.

Selena is from St. Petersburg, Florida, and seems almost angelic with her lithe figure, porcelain skin, and long white-blonde hair. Brook is a Rubenesque woman from Los Angeles, with rosy cheeks, a dewy complexion, silken long brown hair, and a wise, maternal vibe. The room pulsates with shimmery energy like a radiant light shines through each woman. I softly shake my head. My imagination must be running wild. *Trippy.*

Within minutes of talking with them, it becomes clear that I don't control the conversation. It's all I can do to keep from bursting into tears or nervous laughter as they tell me things about myself that they can't possibly know, things that I haven't ever told anyone and that only someone who is an "intuitive" could know.

Selena gazes at me and seems to take in my aura around me. "You want to live a life of connection with spirit, but you fear the judgment of others if you are vulnerable and open about your metaphysical beliefs."

Brook nods, adding, "Dear Kee Kee, you've always felt like a fraud in Hollywood. You've never thought you belonged."

Starr explains. "Kee Kee, being an old soul stuffed into a young body isn't always a pleasant experience. But if you're brave enough to see yourself, you'll lose your fear of living authentically. The more you trust, the brighter your light will shine."

The few times in my life that I have been to so-called psychics, I did it for pure entertainment value. I've always considered myself a realist, grounded in the material world while going along with socially accepted norms. As far as I know, the social norm doesn't embrace advice from soothsayers.

Starr continues. "Your guides are telling me that your soul drew you to Hot Springs for a reason. You need healing."

Okay, yes, clearly, I do. I started my road trip hoping to welcome change in my life and find shama. Wait, *my guides are telling her I need healing?* (What are my "guides," anyway?) Art could have told her about what I shared with him yesterday in the Quapaw Baths and my reasons for driving around the country. Besides, doesn't everyone need healing on some level?

"You are a bridge," declares Starr. Looking first at Selena and then at Brook, she asks, "Don't you think Kee Kee is a bridge?"

They nod in agreement.

"What's a bridge?" I ask.

Selena answers, "It means you can effectively communicate spiritual concepts to people grounded in the material world. You are comfortable navigating both spirit and matter."

This sorta makes sense. I've long nourished two different aspects of my life. I have friends from my involvement with the LA yoga, Buddhist, and spiritual communities, and friends from the film business and everyday activities. I've always been comfortable in both worlds.

My eyes travel from Starr to Selena to Brook. Is it possible to believe in the power of what they do (uh, like talking to spirit guides) without having to sell my soul? Can I process their prophecy and move forward through life with free will?

The next words out of Starr's mouth are, "Your dog is in your 'mate' space."

Ouch.

I hadn't told Art that I have a dog, and Starr refers to a dog before I tell her that Yoda is waiting for me outside in Princess Leia the Prius. I laugh nervously as a swell of panic bubbles up. The back of my throat burns, and my heart races. What if it's true? Am I destined to live a life alone, just Yoda and me? Well, here's the thing: If there is such a thing as a "mate space," then right now, Yoda is most definitely in it. With everything in my life in flux, he's the only constant. When everything else has failed me, my dog hasn't. So maybe she's right?

She mentions accurately how I recently had a dream that Yoda was a man who embodied all the flawless traits of my perfect mate.

Starr goes one step further when she says, "You're being called to write. Through your writing, you will learn to heal yourself."

Selena and Brook say they "see" the same thing.

They invite me to go out to dinner, but I decline. Overwhelmed, stunned, and slightly confused, I look at the three women and say, "It was so good to meet you all. Thank you for the, uh, illuminating conversation. I have to get back to my dog." I don't mention that a certain park ranger and I are meeting for a quick dinner during his break.

Starr softly holds me back as I gather up my crossbody messenger bag to leave. "I'd like to talk with you alone tomorrow morning, before you leave town."

After hesitating for a beat, I think, *What harm can be done in coming back tomorrow for one last conversation with Starr?* I say goodbye to Selena and Brook, who are flying back to their respective homes in the morning, and promise Starr I'll swing by tomorrow. *What am I getting myself into?*

Sam chose Subway for dinner because his break is only thirty minutes. He gives me a bear hug when I walk in.

"Ouch, you're crushing my chest. How do you breathe in that thing?"

"Oh no, I forgot I'm wearing my bulletproof vest," he chuckles.

Sam is leaving for a month-long vacation tonight after his shift, so we promise to keep in touch. We've quickly transitioned to a friend vibe, which is interesting given we spent the past two nights together *au naturel* in a moonlit hotel room. I'm grateful to have met him, and we part ways without expecting anything further between us.

When Yoda and I return to The Arlington, I soak in my room's mineral spring bathtub for a long time, so long that I'm shivering and have puckered fingers and toes by the time I climb out. Dazed and lost in my thoughts, I try to make sense of the things Starr, Brook, and Selena told me. The blunt force of Starr's words is strangely attractive and frightening. It's chilling to hear someone call out my BS, scary to think that I have been blind to my BS, and petrifying to think of the dramatic changes that need to happen to get rid of my BS. By toppling down all I have built for myself, am I drafting a new blueprint for the future? Perhaps this chapter of my life is about finding the balance between mustering up the courage to take steps forward into the unknown while having the patience to let things naturally unfold.

Crawling under the fluffy comforter in bed, I snuggle up to Yoda's warm body (maybe Starr was right about him being in my "mate" space?) and then stare at the ceiling for hours before drifting off to sleep.

In the morning, after I've checked out of the hotel and loaded up Princess, we head over to The Dome. This time, Starr and Art have invited Yoda inside to meet their dogs: Jester, the bullmastiff, and Bosco, the Jack Russell-Chihuahua mix. I'm relieved to have the dogs as an icebreaker because I'm nervous about spending time alone with Starr. Eventually, we head to her office, followed by all three dogs. Seated in office chairs facing each other, we're so close that our knees are almost touching.

She takes my hands in hers, looks into my eyes, and says gently, "Kee Kee, you must stay longer so I can work with you. You must learn to use your uniqueness as hand lotion, not sandpaper."

Use my uniqueness as sandpaper? My mind scrambles to translate her metaphor. *Have I been resisting celebrating my unique bits while instead attempting to conform? Is Starr saying that's why my life has felt so abrasive?*

"Your spirit guides are doing handsprings to get my attention," she proclaims. "They are saying that you need to write, and I need to kick-start the process. We need to dig into the framework of your soul."

I'm listening. To Starr. Who is listening to my "guides."

In that squawky voice of hers, she declares, "I need to stick a lightning bolt up your ass to get you writing and to help you go to places where you wouldn't necessarily otherwise go. If you don't allow yourself to write now, it will be many lifetimes before you heal your psychic wounds and complete what you are destined to do."

I'm tempted to roll my eyes, yet I'm also unnerved because *who the hell wants to carry around psychic wounds?* If what Starr says is true, if I don't stay and work with her, will I be messing up the divine order of my destiny and instead be adding more ingredients to the karmic soup I've spent lifetimes cooking on a slow simmer?

If my spirit guides are talking to her, what private, deep secrets are they sharing? What if they've told her something embarrassing and mortifying about me? Maybe she knows secret things, like how when I get angry or frustrated, I get in my car by myself, without Yoda, and let out a primal scream to release toxic emotions. I feel naked and completely exposed right now.

"Baby, you need to write. Through your writing, you will heal yourself."

Goosebumps spring up on my forearms, and my heart surges into my throat. I feel the truth in her words. Through my recent blogging during my travels, I have quickly learned that, well, it hurts if I don't have time to write each day. What if I stayed in Hot Springs for a while with the sole intention of writing? I could think of it as a journal-writing workshop that might bring about that elusive shama for which I've been searching. Is this idea crazy? Or is it a golden opportunity to find inner peace?

Starr smiles at me. "I've arranged for you to move into the guest bedroom of our dear friend Joanna."

She isn't making it easy to say no. I won't have to pay for lodging, and I can continue to hike in the glorious Hot Springs mountains and soak in the divine thermal baths. One more thing.

I tell her, "I don't believe in gurus, and I don't believe in having only one teacher."

To my relief, Starr responds, "I have no desire to be your guru. All I want to do is light a fire in you so you will write and heal yourself."

Good answer. I agree. "Well, what the heck. I'll stay."

"Good," she says, handing me a red-covered, lined spiral notebook.

When I open it, I see the pages are completely blank.

"I've put a sacred grid on this notebook."

My arm hairs stand on end. I don't know what that is, but it sounds important. Anyone who knows how to put a sacred grid on something, whatever that is, and if it is even possible, is someone I want on my team.

"I made the grid on the notebook with Light Language, a practice that stems from the ancient Mayans and Aztecs," she explains. "It creates healing by using colored light and sacred geometry."

I've heard about sacred geometry in my Santa Monica yoga community. It involves ascribing sacred meanings to repeating symmetrical patterns in the natural world, like how fingerprint spirals mimic galaxies and age rings in a tree stump, and how pinecones and seashells are like the spiral-shaped foliage of a Begonia Escargot. Branching trees are like leaf veins, blood vessels, and the tributaries of a meandering river. Then there's the hypnotic self-repeating pattern in Romanesco broccoli and frost crystals.

Starr continues. "Light Language comes from a long, unbroken lineage of Mexican curanderos. After many years of study in Mexico, I returned to the United States with the teachings."

She hands me a pen and tells me to open the notebook.

"What about your life are you angry about?"

"Oh, I'm not angry. Just pretty sad these days."

"Bullshit, Kee Kee. Tell me the things that make you angry, and then write them down."

Am I angry? I start to write. Slowly, at first. Once I get going, the emotion rises to the surface, and I press my pen hard onto the paper as I scribble out the many reasons behind my anger, saying and writing:

- I left Hollywood angry.
- There is so much more to life than making movies.
- People in Hollywood can be so insecure that they seek fame, power, and money to validate their worth.
- Hollywood thinks it is the most important industry in the world.

- People feel inadequate when they compare themselves to actors, who are some of the most screwed-up people I know.
- *I'm angry with myself for staying in an unfulfilling life for so long.*

When I say the last one and write it down, I stop talking as I look down at the paper. I've written so fast that the words are almost illegible. Oh my God, I'm not angry at Hollywood. I am angry with myself. I've let *myself* down! I put a career I haven't cared about ahead of living a life that brings me joy. Hollywood isn't the problem; I am.

I look up at Starr. "I'm a goody two-shoes. I've been afraid to live my life for me. That's what I'm most angry about."

She lets out a hearty laugh. "Yes, you are a fucking goody two-shoes." She clearly saw this exercise as a way to realize that for myself. "It's good you found your way to me. It's time for Goody Two-Shoes to get real," she clucks, with a sparkle in her eye.

I consider her words. Having been so strict with living the way I thought I was supposed to, does that mean I haven't been real? If Starr can help me, I'm ready to do the work. "I want to get real!"

"Great." Starr swivels in her chair and reaches up to the light switch to turn off the bright overhead light. She turns to me and demands, "Now, hold my hands and look into my eyes."

We clasp hands, our knees are touching, and she locks eyes with me. She's staring intently into my eyes.

"Smile inwardly, Kee Kee. Small movements in your facial muscles can affect your perception."

I know what she's talking about. I've seen photos of myself without that tiny uplift in my cheeks, and I look tired, dour, and old. Coercing a subtle inner smile, I meet her eyes. I try not to blink since she's not, but the thought makes me blink more.

"Tell me what you see."

I'm sure I know what she wants me to say—that I'm looking into her eyes and seeing a reflection of my soul? It's supposed to be a spiritual awakening where I realize I am one tiny grain of sand that's part of an entire beach, or one little wave that's part of the whole ocean. I'm supposed to lose my sense of Self and instead be at one with the world. Yet none of that happens. Instead, I "see" a peculiar, plump woman starting to freak me out. It's dark in the room, and I need to give her an answer. "I see shadows."

She sighs. "We have some work ahead of us."

I think I flunked this one.

She dismisses me. "That's it for today. Go to Joanna's house now and come back tomorrow for lunch. You can bring Yoda again. The dogs like him."

For some unknown reason, I'm letting this woman boss me around.

Art enters and hands me a small portable air purifier. "You'll want this for the bedroom."

I leave The Dome with directions to Joanna's house. When we arrive, I park on the street and sit in my car in front of her home and call the Memphis hotel where I booked this morning. I'm relieved that I can cancel without penalty. I feel bewildered and drained from the experience with Starr. With Yoda on his leash, I collect myself, walk to the front door, and knock.

Joanna opens the door and holds back her large Rottweiler while she says hello. *Crap, she has a Rottweiler?* Joanna is a silver-haired woman in her late sixties with a raspy voice and an unsteady gait due to a bad hip.

"Don't worry, April loves dogs," she says.

I take a deep breath—*yes, but does she also love people?* Joanna invites me in and gives me a quick tour of her house. The living room has a forest-green carpet and a cloud of smoke in the air. *Great, Joanna is a smoker.* A chain smoker who constantly has a cigarette in her hand even though she has a persistent hacking cough. Thank goodness the guest bedroom has two windows I can crack for fresh air. *Hey Art, thanks for the air purifier. I get it now.*

Joanna has an early dinner ready for us. We sit at the table and get to know each other while we eat her savory homemade stew filled with chunky root vegetables and fresh herbs. It is so delicious that I hold out my bowl when Joanna asks if I want more. April nudges my hand, looking up at me with big doe eyes and drooling from the smell of the food. I've never met a Rottweiler and have always thought them to be mean, territorial guard dogs. Yet April is gentle and insists on sleeping with me and Yoda, giving me as many kisses as she can before I say, "Enough, April," and she starts licking Yoda's face.

The following day, I arrive in time for lunch at The Dome and chug the last of my coffee as I park. Starr is in the dining area, sitting at a table with a familiar willowy woman.

"Hi, Kee Kee!" says the woman in her soft voice, surprised to see me after Art's introduction at the Quapaw Baths.

"Melissa! I'm so happy to see you." *The world gets smaller!*

"And you as well. I'm staying in town for a week of intensive study with Starr."

Starr dishes up a salad for lunch while the three of us talk.

My inner yogi is thrilled to be getting to know Melissa. I explain how refreshing it is to be out in real America, away from the bubble of Hollywood. "In LA, I need sunglasses to see through the bling," I lament. "But none of that matters on the open road. I'm learning so much about myself and life."

When we finish eating, Starr says, "Melissa is here for the next few days, and I'll be spending most of my time with her," and hands me two workbooks that she authored. "This first week you'll be completing written exercises in the workbooks and checking in with me."

Apparently, I'm going back to school. The first workbook is *FASTtrack: the workbook to get out of your own way FAST!*, and the second is called *DEEPtrack: the workbook to clear soul scars.*

Starr is staring at me, or rather, right through me.

"I'm doing something to you," she says.

I'm bemused. Am I supposed to believe Starr is casting a magic spell on me? While this process lasts only about twenty seconds, it feels like an hour. I fidget while glancing at Melissa. *What have I gotten myself into?*

Starr instructs, "Now go for a long hike before you go home. You may get sick later."

Completely mystified about what has transpired, I'm slightly dumbfounded that I'm so willing to take orders from, dare I say, a metaphysical woo-woo weirdo. Nonetheless, Yoda and I head out for that long hike. *Me, sick? I feel great.* We hike for two hours on the forest trails. When we reach Hot Springs Mountain Tower, I sit on a bench while Yoda lies down, panting at my feet. I pour water from my bottle into his collapsible bowl, and he eagerly laps it up while I lap up the view. The valley below is expansive, with iridescent beams of afternoon sunlight filtering through the clouds like God's fingers reaching down from the heavens.

I tie my long hair into a knot on my head, enjoying the soft breeze that cools the beads of sweat on the back of my neck. Inhaling so deeply that my lungs tingle with the refreshing December air, I reflect on how my road trip has taken such a strange and unexpected turn.

I've been a seeker for as long as I can remember, so transfixed by hope for something more to life, that I had to find meaning; living without understanding my life and the reasons for being here left me feeling my life had no weight. My endless search left me with more questions than answers. Being a type A, perfectionist, analytical woman with a worrying nature, having no answers became the bane of my existence. Compounding the problem was that my rule-following nature means I've always been afraid of straying too far from what I deemed a socially acceptable path to go find those answers. The menial tasks of everyday living always strapped me: paying bills, returning work phone calls, booking the oil changes, and shopping for groceries. I never had room in the schedule for something as extravagant as a spiritual quest to an ashram in India.

Traditional resources didn't help answer any of my heavy questions. No textbook, teacher, television show, or conversation with friends revealed the purpose of life. So, I turned to explorations of the world's religions and spiritual philosophies, desperate to find a string of peace threaded through my constant search for a meaningful existence.

Baptized Catholic and raised Lutheran, I was very involved with church in my youth. The problem is that although I found the community and church ritual enjoyable, I didn't know if I believed in Christianity. I didn't necessarily *not* believe, but at the same time couldn't say that I truly did believe, since I didn't understand. I don't trust without questioning what confuses me, and many Bible teachings don't make sense.

During college, when I became a conversational English tutor, I eagerly dug through a stack of applications from international students. Nai-Sher's application stood out head and shoulders above the rest because he wrote that he'd be able to teach his tutor about Taoism, Buddhism, and astrology. That sold me. In 1993, Nai-Sher was a Taiwanese PhD candidate who wanted to practice his English. Today, Nai-Sher is an accomplished mathematics professor in Taipei.

The first time I met Nai-Sher, I noticed his gentleness. He was lean and fit and moved with a poetic grace. He had an air of contentment about his life, and his compassionate eyes reflected wisdom—wisdom I desperately wanted him to share. The job of a conversational English tutor is to, well, converse. So, I asked him how his practices of Taoism, Buddhism, and astrology helped him understand the meaning of life and how these practices could help me find my place in this world.

By the time I moved to Chicago for law school, the roles of tutor and student had blurred, and Nai-Sher had become a treasured friend. Using some of the techniques he taught me, I started to meditate. We also continued our conversations over the phone, during which I would express my angst about my purpose in life and my frustration that I didn't understand. Nai-Sher would tell me to be patient and be in the moment.

Living for today was never anything I was any good at. I was always working toward the future, trying to stick to my *plan* for my life, whether it pleased me or not. The plan was to get good grades in law school, have a successful career, fall madly in love, get married, have children, and live happily ever after in a big house on the beach. My plan didn't involve deviating very far from the social norm, meaning I never thought long and hard about what would truly make *me* happy.

At that point, I wasn't committed to my meditation practice. Meditation was boring and seemed lazy—my mind chattered louder than ever, asking why I was sitting with my eyes closed when I should be doing something productive. When I moved to Los Angeles, I discovered yoga, which suited me better because yoga is meditation in motion. I was doing something while still quieting my mind. Yoga logically led to a desire to learn more about yoga philosophy, so I went through yoga teacher training. Then, I took evening classes in Eastern philosophy at Loyola Marymount University.

My searching verged on manic. Convinced I needed to learn everything I could about every religion and spiritual practice to find the buried truth, I couldn't identify with any one practice.

Then, one night, I picked up a book that had been sitting on my nightstand for a month. It had a toilet on the cover, and the title was *Hardcore Zen: Punk Rock, Monster Movies and the Truth about Reality*, written by a punk rock musician named Brad Warner from Akron, Ohio. He had moved to Japan to make monster movies and, in the process, became a Zen priest.

Brad's writing spoke to me. Instead of using the ubiquitous esoteric language that most spiritual books use—the type that has me reading a paragraph four times before admitting I still don't know what it means—Brad writes in the commonplace language of the West. Foul language, taboo topics, sex, self-deprecation—nothing is off-limits. He tells readers to question everything, not to believe him, and instead figure it out for themselves. He doesn't want to be put on a pedestal because he says he's one of us. His book was different from any other spiritual book I had ever read.

I stayed up late into the night, reading the entire book. In the morning, I found Brad's email address in Japan and wrote to him, saying how profoundly his book affected me. I asked to be put on his email list should he ever hold a retreat in the USA. An hour later, I received an email back from him. He had moved to LA the week before and was looking for a place to teach Zen Buddhism—did I know of anywhere? Indeed, I did.

That is how, over a decade after Nai-Sher introduced me to Buddhism, I finally started to practice. Every Saturday, I would gather with Brad's sangha and sit on a meditation cushion facing the wall for an hour. Finally, the process of meditation started to make sense to me.

Brad is certainly unlike anyone I ever expected to call a spiritual teacher. He wears punk rock T-shirts and has a plastic Godzilla on the altar alongside a Buddha statue and burning incense. Brad doesn't want to be called a teacher. Yet they say when the student is ready, the teacher will appear. Brad appeared when I needed him, landing right in my lap the morning after I read his book. Over the years, he has also become a friend.

Through Zen meditation, called zazen, and my studies of Zen Buddhism, I began to understand that there is truth in absolutely everything. Sometimes, I wish I had it in me to throw my faith into one belief system, but that isn't my path. I now find bits and pieces of answers in Christianity, Hinduism, Yoga Philosophy, Taoism, Judaism, Islam, Buddhism—essentially finding truth in everything. What I believe is a mixture of it all. Now, here I am in Hot Springs, Arkansas, getting a crash course in metaphysics, a fascinating mix of science, philosophy, and religion.

How in the world could I accurately describe to anyone this experience with Starr? Will my friends think I've lost my mind to agree to stay here and "work" with a complete stranger? Will I even have the courage to tell anyone? It doesn't escape me that the hesitation stems from my old pattern of being afraid of living by my own rules. One thing I do know is that I'm already having fun with this adventure. Before this road trip, it had been so long since I'd had excitement in my life, and hey, isn't this what I asked for? To go willingly and spontaneously into the unknown. Kind of like *Star Trek*, but not into outer space, more like inner space.

SEVENTEEN

Hot Springs — A Guy

Meanwhile, back on Earth, before I return to Joanna's house, I stop at Kroger and load up on groceries to share with her. Back at her place, I gather an armload of logs from the backyard woodpile. Joanna sits in her armchair while I set up the paper and kindling to start a fire in the fireplace. I tell her about what happened at The Dome.

A long-practicing metaphysicist, she explains, "Starr gave you a download, Kee Kee," as she exhales a mouthful of cigarette smoke.

Me: quietly coughing.

Joanna continues. "A download is when you receive a menagerie of information from a master teacher when you're ready to receive it. You can use it for your highest good. As needed, your subconscious mind will bring this information to your conscious mind." Joanna stubs out her cigarette in a large vintage brass ashtray. "She told you to go for a hike because getting out in nature helps you process and integrate the download where you have fewer distractions."

I am grateful to be here for her to translate this new language for me. I ask her, "What if I don't want that information in my brain? Does it go there without my permission?" I'm concerned that someone can just deposit information into my brain whether I want it there or not.

"A download can only happen when a person makes an agreement with a teacher on the soul level to receive this information. It's like a computer download. The master teacher makes the information available to be downloaded. If the soul accepts, then the download starts flowing into one's subconscious."

The crazy thing is, I'm hoping what Joanna is saying is true. Who wouldn't want to be given information from a master teacher to use for their highest good? This is the closest thing to winning the lottery.

I have another question. "Why doesn't Starr tell me this information? That seems a lot easier than whatever she does to muster up the power to send it to me telepathically."

Joanna lights up another cigarette. "A download is valuable because the conscious mind can handle five pieces of information per minute, whereas the subconscious mind can handle ten thousand pieces of information per minute. It's all about free will—a person will not receive a download unless that person wants it."

I'm wary of her statistics, but I get the idea. I still have so many questions. Did I want the download? Did Starr and I agree on the soul level? Maybe when I accepted her offer of help, that was my agreement. The sky's the limit now!

After the fire starts crackling, Yoda and I settle in on the sofa next to Joanna's oversized puffy recliner. She could get lost in that thing. I sneeze. Then cough.

"I'm sorry, smoke makes me wheeze." I wave away cigarette smoke that is floating in my direction.

Joanna says she thinks I am getting sick.

Yeah, sick of cigarette smoke.

"Your body is dense, so when you start to process the information in a download, sometimes you will fall ill because you have so much erroneous information and patterns to release. Getting sick is a way to get it out of you quickly so light has space to move in and go where it needs to go."

This is getting complicated.

What's curious is that I'm giving serious consideration to the things people are saying instead of automatically writing everyone off as crackpots.

Later, I wake up in a pool of sweat while simultaneously shivering. My muscles ache, and my chest rattles as I wheeze and cough. Is this the flu or a side effect of Starr's download? I don't care. All I know for sure is that I am sick, and I'm a terrible houseguest to become bedridden the second day I'm at Joanna's house. When I call Starr to explain why I won't be able to make it over, she tells me to spend the next few days getting healthy while I work through the exercises in the two workbooks.

Joanna makes me homemade chicken rice soup, and Yoda and I alternate between the bed and sofa for three days while I complete the written exercises in the workbooks. Yoda is the perfect dog to have around when I'm not feeling well. He's content to spend heavenly lounging hours nestled against me. April often hops up on the bed and joins him for long naps.

When I first open the workbooks, I'm worried the metaphysical hocus-pocus will ensnare me. However, the essays I'm writing in response to the written questions are penetrating and insightful. To me, anyway. I'm writing about early life experiences that have defined me as an adult, and the written exercises are helping me confront my demons. I'm tackling meaning-of-life issues that I barely made a dent in during previous years of therapy, which now seem like a waste of time and money.

One of the exercises in *DEEPtrack* asks me to list my emotional soul choices that came in with me into this lifetime, as well as those learned from my environment as part of my soul contract.

- I am sensitive to noise, large groups of people, and chaos.
- I am a closet loner and need time alone to recharge.
- I am deeply introspective.
- I fight the urge to be passive-aggressive.
- I am sensitive, easily moved by emotion, and easily having my feelings hurt.
- I feed off others' energy and absorb it.

Then the workbook asks me why these emotional soul choices were part of my soul contract and which soul lessons I choose to learn from them. I let the words flow without censoring them, and when I read them back out loud, I feel an aha about my life.

- I needed these soul choices to lead me to learn to listen to my inner voice.
- I needed these soul choices to bring me to the point I'm at now, being open to spirit instead of getting lost in materialism, status, parties, and social nonsense.
- I needed these soul choices to give me the ability to connect one-on-one with others deeply.
- I choose to learn that I need not judge myself for not enjoying large crowds and that true rewards are found by connecting with people in small groups.
- I choose to learn not to absorb others' energy negatively.
- I choose to learn not to take things personally and not to let my feelings get hurt.

It may be some time before I truly embody these choices, but verbalizing them seems a strong step in the right direction. I sit in bed with my computer on my lap and take a break from my homework to check my email. There's a message sent through my new blog from someone named Mathias. He's a Houston artist who posted a photo of a napkin sketch of an *American Gothic*-inspired house on his blog. He said he found *my* comment on his blog about living in the real American Gothic House. I bet Beth commented on his blog because she receives Google Alerts about the American Gothic House.

He said he found me by searching online for "Who lives in the American Gothic House?" My blog popped up because I had written about recently visiting Beth. He must have only skimmed my post and assumed I live there.

Mathias' email is short and slightly formal, thanking me for "my comment." I send him a cheeky email telling him that Beth lives there and I am her friend who is having an existential crisis while driving across the country with my dog, trying to find inner peace.

Mathias immediately responds. Last year, he took a road trip with his dog across the Southwest. His marriage had ended, he had to file for bankruptcy, and he plummeted into a deep depression. His solution, like mine, was to drive and see where the road took him. Yet now he writes that he is content with his life and grateful for the changes he made because of hitting rock bottom.

His story is so like mine. This faceless stranger tells me he went through what I'm going through and surfaced on the other side as a better, happier man. He writes that it took losing almost everything for him to realize that happiness stems from the simple things in life, like family, home-cooked meals, and healthy friendships.

Something about this man makes me want to pour out my story to him. Sometimes, it's easier to open up to people I don't know, and here is a stranger to whom I can freely write. If he judges me, it doesn't matter because we don't know each other.

We send each other emails each day with short, flirty, bullet-point facts about ourselves at the end of each one. Some witty, some cutesy, some deep.

From Mathias to me:
- *green eyes change color with my mood*
- *pet pug with cartoonishly long legs*
- *divorced, my fault*
- *pain is poetry*

From me to Mathias:
- *I can wiggle my ears*
- *had braces three times*
- *never married*
- *I named my car*

Mathias has my attention, and his emails are a nice distraction from being bedridden with my mystery illness.

When I finally feel well enough to return to The Dome, Starr tells me it's time to start writing exercises applicable solely to me. Using my red-covered spiral notebook (the one infused with her magic grid of light), she lists a beginning outline of essay ideas to write down. We will pick a topic each day for me to write about. Her brainstorming of subjects includes things like *Ten Things I Want to Heal in Myself, How I Hid My Real Self in Corporate America, My Rites of Passage — All My First Experiences, What is My Separation Anxiety from God?, Why Am I So Afraid to Be Vulnerable?,* and *If I Keep Moving, What Am I Running From?*

Each day, I meet with Starr, and true to her word, she cracks her whip. I spend hours writing. She helps me dredge up memories I had long forgotten and develop the courage to write about experiences I never dreamed I'd have the nerve to share. The process is painful, raw, and, at the same time, exhilarating. I'm finally severing cords that connect me to past events and people who have only served to hold me back in life.

Sometimes, she makes me rewrite essays three or four times, telling me something is missing and to dig deeper. I usually resist, only realizing later that she was right. By her pushing me, I remember an important tidbit that I need to include, which she'll read and say, "Yes, *now* you got it."

Eager to please Starr, I'm worried that I won't meet her expectations with my writing or that she has erroneously seen something in me that doesn't exist. I worry that I'm a fraud, pretending to be a writer, so I don't let Starr down by not fulfilling her prophecy that I will heal myself through writing.

Each day after leaving The Dome, I rush back to Joanna's house to my computer to see if there is an email waiting from Mathias. It's always there. Mathias has started sending me a photo every morning. Sometimes, he has bed head, and other times, he's dressed for work. He is deliciously handsome, with tousled wavy blond hair, a square jaw, light scruff, perfect teeth, and piercing green eyes. Mathias's emails are a welcome break from the intensity of my "homework" for Starr. When I receive another email from Harry, "just checking in," I am surprised at how much more excited I am to receive Mathias's emails. A man I've never met is somehow helping me wake up from the fairy-tale idea of Harry and me.

I send Beth an email to tell her about Mathias and attach one of the photos he sent me. She calls me when she opens the email.

"Oh Kee Kee, his square jaw is perfect! He seems like a catch."

I laugh. "By moving into the American Gothic House, you may have inadvertently become a matchmaker."

Starr arranges for me to meet several of her friends. One night, I attend an exhibit of an artist who takes photos of faces that she sees in the bark of trees. Another day, I meet a laughing yoga instructor for tea. Today, I'm having lunch with Starr's close friend Joe. She says he and I are meant to be in each other's lives. Joe is a photographer and filmmaker from Portugal who speaks four languages fluently. After living all over the world, he now calls Hot Springs home.

I walk into Rolando's, a restaurant in an 1800s-era building with colorful Ecuadorian art on the walls. It takes a minute for my eyes to adjust from the bright sunlight to the dimly lit room. Joe is waiting at a table in the back of the restaurant. With his long, snow-white beard and his hair tied into a lengthy ponytail, he's a blend of Santa Claus and a wise, ethereal wizard. When he sees me, his smile sparkles and his eyes twinkle, and he greets me with a cheery laugh. I spontaneously say, "I feel such an immediate connection with you!"

With delight, he replies, "I feel a similar connection with you, my spiritual daughter!"

"Then that makes you my Papa Joe," I laugh. "The name quite suits you."

In his lyrical accent, he speaks with poetic sound bites.

I tell Papa Joe how connected I already am to Hot Springs and how I've begun to believe the thermal waters drew me here to teach me something.

"Keep learning from the waters," he instructs. "You can give the old and the negative to the flow of the waters and have them washed away. Use these healing waters to replenish and open your heart to life."

When I mention the deep sadness and frustration that led me to the road, he responds, "Think of life as your classroom and the Universe as your holy book. The days are the holy book's pages, and each moment is a word."

"I had such plans for my life, but they've all fallen away."

"When you focus on your wants instead of your needs, it turns the highway into a parking lot."

Our conversation moves to his photography. His eclectic portfolio includes photos of everyone from presidents of the United States, leaders of other countries, and Pope John Paul II to rock stars and spiritual leaders.

"What inspires your work?" I ask.

"I photograph people's inner light," he says. "When we're in the presence of someone, we don't see each other. We see the modulated light reflecting off the surface of that person."

He smiles at me. "When light shines upon a person, some is absorbed and the rest is reflected. So, I'm looking at your light right now. What I am receiving from you is the gift of your reflected light."

Papa Joe looks at every part of life—the nasty, beautiful, hateful, and loving—as participating in the conscious process of a divine education. We're all interconnected—growing, learning, and evolving into more loving people.

My connection with Papa Joe grows each time I see him over the coming weeks. We walk and eat, and he photographs me as our friendship evolves. When he shows me proofs of the photos he has taken, I remark with surprise, "I thought I'd look road-weary and depressed. I look refreshed and happy!"

"That's because I photographed your light," he says, eyes twinkling.

The vivid dreams about the crystals in the mountains started soon after I met Starr. They are colorful, vibrating, and fill my body with shimmering light. One night, I dream that Starr is talking to me while I sit surrounded by piles of amethysts. I know what she says is important, but I can't understand her words. Sometimes, her mouth is moving, but I can't hear anything. At other times, she's audibly speaking, but it sounds like gibberish. Some nights, I dream that Starr is pressing me emotionally, telling me to be more vulnerable. "Open up and be fully one with your flaws and pain." I'm pushing back, resisting as I grip thumb-sized quartz crystals. She pushes some more and tells me, "You need to break through." Although I don't mention these dreams to anyone, I think about them all day long.

Then, on Christmas Eve, Starr and Art invite Yoda and me over to share a holiday meal. They seem genuinely pleased that we are here. Art hands me a gift bag and says, "Merry Christmas to our new friend, Kee Kee." Inside is a blue mug with a star on it and a brightly colored journal that has a peace symbol on the cover. The front of the greeting card features Yoda (of *Star Wars* fame).

Yoda, Jester, and Bosco lie at our feet while we eat Starr's homemade three-onion soup. Starr looks up from her bowl. "I've been sending you to night school, baby."

Whoa.

Starr continues. "I've been coming to you in your dreams, urging you to have a breakthrough, but you keep resisting me." She puts down her spoon. "I've been showing you the power of crystals, so you can learn from them."

How does she know about my dreams of crystals? Could it be possible that she has been teaching me while my conscious mind sleeps? If so, what's *crystal* clear is that I'm a piss-poor excuse for a student.

Later, when I return to Joanna's, she explains that night school is teaching received in the dream state. Native American teachers have long engaged in what they call Dreamtime Teachings. Since our brains are highly active during REM sleep, we can process much more information while we sleep than when we are awake. Joanna tells me that metaphysicists believe we receive forty hours of teaching for every hour of night school.

On New Year's Day, Joanna's daughter, Paulla, brings over black-eyed peas for lunch. "These peas have been on the stove since six a.m., so the ham should be tender." She sets the pot on a trivet and gives me a pointed look. "You do know that you need to eat black-eyed peas every New Year's Day for good luck, don't you?"

Oh shit, maybe that's where I went wrong.

"Did you hear about the birds?" asks Joanna as she holds up the morning paper. "Thousands of red-winged blackbirds fell from the sky last night in Beebe, about ninety minutes from here. It says they landed on cars and roofs and all over people's lawns."

"That's tragic. Apocalyptic, like a scene out of a horror movie," I exclaim.

"It says they mighta been spooked by fireworks. Could've been scared to death," she says, reading.

"And how about those fish?" asks Paulla.

"What fish?" Lately, I feel naive and sheltered from the news.

"You didn't hear? A couple of nights ago, they found a hundred thousand dead drum fish floating in the Arkansas River."

I almost choke on a black-eyed pea. "Noooo, that's so sad and crazy. I didn't think Arkansas could get any stranger, but the rollercoaster of improbability continues."

"I told you, Kee Kee," says Joanna. "Arkansas is unlike any other place you'll ever visit."

"There sure seem to be surprises around every corner," I say as I look down to see my empty plate when I thought I had at least a few bites of black-eyed peas left. "Well, there's one thing I know for sure. I'm going in for seconds. It's going to be a good year, dammit."

Later on New Year's Day, Starr and I sit on her bed with all three dogs as we look through a pile of semi-precious gemstone rings left over from their annual Christmas party, where Art had hosted the fire walk. Starr had decorated a tree with the rings and told guests to help themselves. She hands me two rings—one with a stone that's a kaleidoscope of colors and another with a large oval green gemstone.

"The aventurine will open your heart chakra, and the rainbow jasper protects you from dark energy and will help you connect to the energies of the Universe," she explains.

I'm never taking these rings off.

Starr surprises me and hands me a flat plate-sized circle of hardened melted wax. It has peaks, valleys, and bubbles and is quite beautiful—in a blobby melted wax sort of way.

"What is this?" I ask.

"It's your wax reading," says Starr. "Generations of women in my family have read wax for people each New Year's Day. It will tell us what will happen in the coming year."

A wax reading!

She explains. "On the first day of every year, I melt wax and pour it on a plate for each of the special people in my life, and this year, I've included you."

"See this peak?" She points to a crest of wax that looks like a wave.

I look closely.

"This crest shows you will have a spiritual epiphany about yourself in February."

That's good news.

She frowns and points to another area of the wax that looks like an indentation with tiny bubbles.

I'm curious what Starr will say next.

"It seems as if you'll have car trouble in July. It won't be an accident, but you'll have issues with your car. Also in July, you will injure your ankle."

"Oh no!" Both hands fly up to cover my mouth.

"It won't be serious, honey, not a break or anything," she reassures, "but you will definitely hurt your ankle in July."

I shudder. *It's going to be seven long months.*

When I return to Joanna's house, I turn on my laptop to check my email. There's a message from Mathias. The subject line reads "Birthday Present?" One of the bullet-point facts about myself at the end of an email was that my birthday is January 8. His email doesn't have anything written in it, but it does have an attachment of a MapQuest map with the driving route marked from Houston to Hot Springs. My heart skips a beat. Mathias is coming to meet Yoda and me.

We email-volley about him coming on January 7, and agree not to talk on the phone before we meet so our voices are a surprise. I will be counting the days for the next week until I meet him.

But the work with Starr doesn't stop just because I'm distracted by a man; if anything, it's getting more intense. Every night, after spending the day with Starr, I sit with Joanna and analyze that day's experiences. Some are magical, others trivial, and all positively affect me. I begin to believe in the truth of downloads.

At times, I can feel Starr giving them to me. During a particularly intense one, my body tingles, and waves of warm energy move through me. It continues for a few minutes. Starr is sitting behind me while I sit reading in a pew in the main room of The Dome. Even though we aren't talking, she is "doing something to me." When I stand up to move across the room, my knees are weak, and the room is spinning.

Our eyes meet, and mine must have a question reflected in them because she smiles and says, "Yes, baby, I gave you a download."

Another time, she warns me that she's going to give me a download that will leave me itchy and feeling as if I want to jump out of my skin during what may be a sleepless night. She tells me not to worry, and I will feel fine in the morning. I leave, eager to experience the effects she's predicted. Nothing happens. Nada. I'm not itchy or jumpy, and I sleep soundly. *Aha! I finally have proof that it's all hocus-pocus.*

When I arrive at The Dome the following day, Starr is sitting at her computer with her back to me.

Before I can even say hello, she says, "It bounced back."

"What bounced back?"

She spins around in her chair and looks at me. "The download. It didn't take. I've been pushing you too hard, and you weren't ready to receive this information."

Even though I arrived ready to challenge the veracity of so-called downloads, I'm disappointed, as if I've failed because one didn't take. I pressure Starr to explain the download process, what she does and feels, and how she has any idea that it didn't take.

Is it intuition, some spiritual being communicating with her, or is it a physical sensation she feels when the download "bounces back"? I'm frustrated that I can't frame the concept of downloads in the language I speak, and that she's not telling me what valuable information is in this download that I'm not receiving.

"The conscious mind isn't capable of understanding. It is knowledge on a much deeper level," she explains.

My intuition—that tickle in my gut—nudges me to pay attention to this juicy stuff. I'm not used to paying attention to my intuition; my default is to tune into my mind. But to listen to my mind, I need to understand.

As if reading my mind, Starr clucks, "Baby, understanding is the booby prize."

EIGHTEEN

Hot Springs — A Community

It's finally January 7. I park the car by a downtown coffee shop and stand outside the front door with Yoda. My phone chirps. It's Mathias, texting to say he's walking his dog, Oliver, and will be here in thirty seconds. I check my hair in the reflection of the window. Mathias saunters around the corner with Oliver, an adorable, skinny little fawn-colored pug with long legs and a squishy face. Mathias is wearing blue and white pinstripe pants, wingtip shoes, and a dark blazer with a green shirt underneath. His pants are a wee bit short—intentionally, of course, to show off his bright blue and yellow striped socks. Not many people could pull off such a mismatched look, but on Mathias, it seems perfectly natural. His sense of style reflects what I've surmised from his emails as his zealous way of living.

When our eyes meet, I blush. We make nervous small talk as the dogs sniff each other and playfully tussle in the parking lot. Could this match be perfect all around?

After coffee, Yoda and I follow Mathias's car to his hotel, where he checks in. Then, he and Oliver hop into Princess, and I give him a driving tour of Hot Springs. His enthusiasm for the architecture on Bathhouse Row is mesmerizing, and I'm hanging on his every word as he educates me about the various styles of the buildings. Yet the physical chemistry between us is sizzling to the point that I would be engrossed in what he said even if he were informing me about farm irrigation techniques.

The next morning, my birthday, we leave Yoda and Oliver at Joanna's with April, and I take Mathias crystal mining, one of my favorite activities in Hot Springs. Afterward, we go out for lunch, enjoying Bloody Marys and tortilla soup. While we sit at the table, he takes my hand and interlaces his fingers in mine.

"Happy Birthday, Kee Kee, I'm happy we finally met." He leans in to kiss me softly. "I wish I didn't have to leave tomorrow."

Me either.

I'm not ready for this dream to end. The heavens aren't ready for it to finish either, because snow starts falling while we eat. By the time we get out to Princess, this rare Arkansas blizzard covers the roads with snow. Cars are fishtailing into ditches, and we pass a few accidents as I carefully drive (in the snow!). His hotel is quite far, so we head to Joanna's house to wait out the snowstorm with her and the dogs.

As we stomp the snow off our shoes, I ask Joanna, "Is it okay if Mathias and Oliver spend the afternoon at your house until the snowplows clear the roads?"

"Snowplows?" she snorts. "We don't have snowplows here. Make yourself comfortable, Mathias. It appears you'll be spending the night."

While Oliver, Yoda, and April euphorically chase one another in the snowy backyard, Mathias, Joanna, and I cook dinner together.

Joanna's house is small, so Mathias sleeps in the guest room with me. I am nervous and doubt I'll sleep at all. But I do, in Mathias' arms. I feel safe and perfectly natural, which is good because we still can't get him to his hotel the next night either. Finally, three days later, the ice and snow on the roads and highways melt, and Mathias can safely return to his work in Houston.

Before he leaves town, we drive to The Dome so he and Starr can meet. She whisks him off to her office to spend some time alone with him while Art and I play with the dogs. When Mathias comes out, Art gives him a tour of The Dome, and Starr holds me back.

"Be careful, honey," she says. "His demons run deep."

Starr's opinion has become important; I'm learning to trust her. But on Mathias, she must be getting a bad read. He's funny, intelligent, kind, and affectionate. I haven't been this excited about a new man in a long time, and her warning perturbs me a little.

I walk Mathias out to his car and kiss him goodbye. I don't know how much longer I'll be in Hot Springs, but before he drives away, I promise him my next stop will be Houston.

Since I'm spending time in this mystical playground, I owe it to myself and to my spiritual growth to explore as many things as possible. I already told Starr I'm open to more than one teacher.

Joanna offers to introduce me to some people. "Would you like to have a guardian angel reading from a minister named Kaela, who runs a church out of her garage?"

Abso-f*in-lutely!

We arrive at a house filled with dusty crystals and newspaper spread all over the carpet for her incontinent cats. A stench of cat pee and cigarette smoke hangs in the air.

Kaela greets us with a friendly smile. She's wearing a black acrylic sweater with a gold ornate design of angel wings woven across her chest. She leads us into her garage, which she has transformed into a church. Framed prints of Jesus and angels line the walls, and a folding table covered with a lace tablecloth sits at the front of the room as a makeshift altar. Crosses, candles, and angel statues sit on the table and shelves lining the walls. About thirty plastic folding chairs are in neat rows.

"Take a seat," Kaela says, handing me a Bible and pointing to the front row of chairs. "Open it up and read out loud whatever words are in front of you. This exercise is how I communicate with your guardian angels."

Joanna sits a few seats away. A cat jumps on her lap, does a few turns, and settles in and purrs contentedly.

Looking at the Good Book on my lap, I can't remember the last time I held a Bible. This one is heavy and weathered with some turned-down page corners, and it looks as if someone once spilled water on a few pages. I delicately open it to a random page and start reading. Not even processing the words coming out of my mouth, my brain is scrambling to figure out how my reading from a Bible might help Kaela communicate with any guardian angels I may or may not have.

Dear God, please let me have at least one guardian angel. It will be so embarrassing if she says that no angels are looking out for me.

Kaela alternates between closing her eyes and writing on a piece of paper. She's mumbling under her breath as if she's in a trance. After about five minutes, Kaela tells me to stop reading. She hands me the "Counseling Profile" she completed while I was reading from the Bible.

"You have ten guardian angels, which is a lot for a person." *Thank you, God. You did me a solid.*

"However, only four are active right now," Kaela explains.

While tempted to joke, "What, are they sleeping on the job?" I bite my tongue.

Nonetheless, my charge of pride to have so many guardian angels is followed almost immediately by a rush of skepticism that guardian angels exist. She tells me the ways each of these angels communicates with me, often through pains or sensations in different parts of my body connected to a particular angel.

"You rank high in percentages of different types of personality perception and spiritual sensitivity."

I nod as though I understand, but I'm clueless as to what she's talking about.

Does everyone end up having similar things written on their Counseling Profiles? The experience with Kaela ranks a ten in entertainment value and a two in feeling authentic. Well, I must admit, I did ask for it.

Next, Joanna invites me to attend her Monday night Metaphysical Women's Group—women who gather each week to discuss what interests them in the metaphysical world. She tells me it will be a treat, because the group includes a woman who channels the Ascended Master Kuthumi. *Uh, who?* Joanna mentioned a handful of people in Hot Springs who supposedly channel various Ascended Masters, and despite wanting to experience all I can, I draw the line and spend the evening with a movie and one of Brenda's bags of gourmet popcorn.

It's a wild contrast to my staid life a few months ago to seriously consider so many beliefs and practices in this metaphysical Disneyland.

Then, Joanna invites me to experience a session with Dr. Joe, a chiropractor from Little Rock. Years ago, Dr. Joe had a mystical experience that gifted him with holy divine healing. Now, he uses this gift with sacred geometry to replace negative emotional patterns with positive thoughts and feelings. Once a month, he visits Hot Springs and conducts healings using Joanna's living room for his appointments. During my session with Dr. Joe, I lay flat on my back on a chiropractic table in the usual location of her coffee table. He places his hands on the soles of my feet, which, he says, is how he communicates with the Divine about me. He silently asks the Divine questions and receives answers by measuring the minuscule changing length of my legs through the soles of my feet.

A tingling sensation hums throughout my body while his hands hold the bottoms of my feet. He tells me that he is removing fractals *(huh?)* from my DNA to bring me back into my Holy Iota, which he says means "all that you are." During my session, after he lets go of my feet, he writes words and draws geometric shapes on a piece of paper, which he tells me to keep under my pillow for the next two weeks. The experience energizes me, and this feeling continues for hours after I leave him. I'm not sure what to think about the session with Dr. Joe. Something happened, but was it real or imagined? What I do know is that I so want to believe that it was real.

Another day, I return to the Ron Coleman Crystal Mine for a couple of hours of crystal mining. I meet Charlotte, a Reiki Master and massage therapist with a doctorate in integrative medicine. Her practice is in a room off the main public store at the mine. While we're talking, she asks if I want to experience a free crystal sound energy healing. Sure! She has me kneel and place my head in the cavity of a five-foot-high amethyst crystal, telling me it will open my crown chakra. She softly strikes a Tibetan singing bowl with a mallet and then runs the mallet around the rim of the bowl until there is a pulsing bell sound and the bowl "sings." When the bowl hits a certain frequency, it vibrates with the amethyst. The physical sensation of the sound vibrating through my body is so intense that it's the only sense I experience. I think of nothing else; I feel nothing else; I hear and see nothing else. I am completely and totally at one with this physical sensation. Afterward, I'm peaceful and relaxed, as if I've had an hour-long massage instead of five minutes of crystal sound energy healing.

I have various other "readings" or "light work" by people in Hot Springs, none of which rings true. The only thing that feels undeniably authentic is my work with Starr.

Even though I constantly try to poke holes in the experiences with her, I'm unsuccessful with each attempt. Time and again, I have mystical experiences with Starr that I can't explain away.

One morning, I open my computer to find a group email from my friend Sahira sent to her close friends. Her message begins with Marianne Williamson's notable quote from her book *A Return to Love* about the importance of letting our light shine.

I skim over the passage and shoot Sahira a quick response, telling her that I miss her. Then I save the writing assignments that I wrote last night on a flash drive, kiss Yoda goodbye (bonus, Joanna is letting Yoda stay with her and April each day, which is saving me buttloads of moolah on doggie daycare), and head out. When I arrive at The Dome, Starr's assistant, Roy Rivers, lets me use his computer to print out my writing assignment to share with Starr.

Roy has quickly become my confidant and hiking partner. He's a talented singer-songwriter whose voice is uncannily similar to John Denver's. His duet with Dolly Parton, "Thank God I'm a Country Boy," shot to Number 1 on the European country charts. He has also received six European CMA award nominations, including Dolly and him winning the 2006 European CMA for Vocal Collaboration of the Year. In between tour schedules, Roy helps Starr. I'm lucky that he's working in her office during my stay in Hot Springs. Our conversations about everyday things—in the mornings in his office, during our many hikes together, or when we go fill our water bottles with crystal-clear mineral water that flows out of the city's five public filling stations—keep me from getting too lost in the massive metaphysical education I'm receiving.

Roy's also an extra incentive for me to attend Starr and Art's Sunday morning church gatherings, because he sings and plays his guitar. At the end of each service, the congregation gathers in a circle, holding hands, and, led by Roy, sings their weekly anthem, "Let There Be Peace on Earth." My knees went weak the first time we sang it, and I stood wide-eyed in shock. Before my road trip, I had never heard this song. Yet I encountered the lyric "Let there be peace on earth, and let it begin with me" on the Internet in the bleak days before Yoda and I took to the road. I was in the darkest of desperate places when I googled "I need inner peace" and stumbled on the song. I added it to my road trip playlist, and by now, this song, which I had never previously heard, has become part of my road trip anthology. Now, here in Hot Springs, Arkansas, a group sings this song every week.

When I mention this miracle to Starr, she smiles and says, "Baby, when will you understand that Hot Springs called your soul here?"

This particular morning doesn't leave time for socializing with Roy before Starr is ready for us to get to work. I hand her my written homework, and she starts reading. About halfway through, she abruptly stops, raises her eyebrows, and looks up.

"Let's talk about the Marianne Williamson quote."

"Huh?" I slightly remember the quote at the beginning of Sahira's email.

"You need to go home and re-read that part of the email you received," she says.

I'm stunned as I gape at her with my mouth open. "Did you just pull that out of my head?" I ask, astonished.

"Yes, it's floating around in there and it applies directly to you. You didn't give it enough attention, so you have to go back and read it again," she says, lecturing me in her squawky voice.

I swallow hard. I look down at my hands, which I'm squeezing together so tightly in my lap that I can feel beads of perspiration forming between my palms. The veins on the tops of my hands bulge out, blue from the blood pulsing through them. Is she privy to any other secrets that are floating around in the deep recesses of my mind? Then it occurs to me: I've been searching for this form of "proof."

I hesitate a moment longer, then glance up and quietly utter, "Thank you for doing that. I've been looking for something I can't explain away."

She softly responds, "Baby, I'd do it a lot more often, but I can't risk you getting scared and running away."

A few hours later, Roy and I are hiking to Balanced Rock, a large boulder seemingly precariously balanced on its end. When Roy and I met, I felt I'd made a friend for life, which is why I dragged him on a hike to help me analyze the day's events.

After telling him about Starr seemingly reading my mind this morning, I ask, "Roy, I feel I'm losing my mind. Can my experiences with Starr really be real? I've spent my life in a fierce tug-of-war between two aspects of my mind, one that desperately wants to believe in the metaphysical and one that wants to remain in the safe, protective bubble of realism. Is there a force greater than our mortal minds can comprehend? Or is the only reality the one we interact with using our five senses?"

My questions echo in the air as we reach the hike's summit. Roy grabs my hand to help me climb to the top of Balanced

Rock. We stand beside each other overlooking a sweeping view of the lush, green Ouachita Mountains. A hawk flies directly in our line of sight. Suddenly, intense vertigo waves through me, and I clutch Roy's arm to steady myself. He helps me sit down on the flat top of the boulder and then plops down next to me.

"Balanced Rock is one of the seven energy vortexes in Hot Springs," he explains.

I laugh. "Of course it is! I'm caught in an 'energy vortex' while trying to explain away my metaphysical experiences."

"Sometimes we have to accept what is, without trying to analyze it to pieces." Roy gives my shoulder a reassuring squeeze. "Don't worry. It gets easier with time."

I'm not sure if he's talking about my vertigo from the vortex or about accepting the truth in my metaphysical experiences with Starr.

Having spent a month in Hot Springs, I can feel myself changing. Starr has shown me that, as the quote from Pierre Teilhard de Chardin says, I'm not a human being searching for a spiritual experience. It's the other way around. We are all spiritual beings having a human experience. Locking away painful parts of my human experience will not help me grow. With Starr's guidance, writing and working through these things has made me feel lighter and happier than I've been in years.

So, I am gripped with emotion when Starr announces one day that our work together is done for now. Part of me is sad that I'm leaving, and the other part is excited because the next stop on the road is to see Mathias in Houston.

Before I leave town, I attend church at The Dome. At the closing of the service, Roy strums his guitar as everyone stands in a circle holding hands, singing "Let There Be Peace on Earth" while we sway from side to side in unison. Gulping back tears so hard that I can't squeak out a word of the song, I look around the circle with love and gratitude at all the now familiar faces.

I've learned so much from this community at a time in my life when I needed them. It's not easy saying goodbye to the many new friends I've made during my stay in Hot Springs—Art, Joanna, Papa Joe, Roy, and many others. However, I find it the most challenging to part ways with Starr. With her naughty sense of humor and profanity-laced insights, this woman has selflessly shared compassion, love, friendship, and wisdom. She's helped me open doors in my spirit that I didn't realize needed opening, and didn't even know existed.

Despite my initial skepticism, Starr's been right all along: my latest lesson of the road is that writing heals me. It's not the crystals, guardian angels, or downloads; my words have the power. Whether journaling, writing a letter, blogging, or emailing my thoughts to a friend, I know I will let the words flow for the rest of my life.

NINETEEN

Houston and New Orleans

After more than seven hours on the road, we finally arrive. As I park Princess outside Mathias's apartment building, I feel a flutter in my chest and a slight swooning sensation. Yoda picks up on my energy, stands in the back seat, and makes a yodel-whine noise when Mathias walks out the front entrance. After greeting us, Mathias sweeps me into his arms, where I melt and remain for twelve hours.

The next day, we only leave the apartment to walk Yoda and Oliver. Otherwise, we spend our time in bed, watching movies and drinking wine. He also cooks for me.

"Watching you cook makes me think you're as much a genius in the kitchen as you are in the bedroom," I say, sitting on a bar stool at the counter, wearing his dress shirt as a robe.

He laughs. "Darlin', behold my masterpiece." He ceremoniously sets a plate of food in front of me with a bow.

He has "whipped up" roasted Cornish hen stuffed with smoked sausage, garlic, onion, sweet potatoes, and tomato confit, alongside a savory duck soup spiced with cumin and curry.

I moan with the first mouthful. "Have you always cooked like this? These dishes are amazing."

"Thank you! Cooking is a new skill in my repertoire. Losing all my money through my divorce didn't mesh well with my appetite for dining out on expensive gourmet meals. So, I started experimenting in the kitchen. I still surprise myself when I intuitively know which spices blend in complementary ways. It's like art class."

Mathias approaches his cooking the same way he approaches his art—with passion, creativity, and improvisation.

When we finally leave the house the next day, I reach for my credit card and groan—it's not there. I know where I lost it. When driving to Houston, I stopped for gas, putting my credit card in my back pocket after I swiped it (I distinctly recall thinking that was a bad idea). I stopped at a rest stop later, where it must have slid out of my pocket. Sure enough, my credit card company confirms that someone found my card in the rest stop, and they have already cancelled it. I give them Mathias's address to send a new card, although they can't guarantee when it will arrive. Similarly to when Mathias was stranded with me in Hot Springs due to the snow, I am now stranded with him in Houston due to the loss of my credit card.

When my card still hasn't arrived five days later, the credit card company tells me it appears FedEx lost the package, so they will have to send another one. It's as if the heavens want us to be together. We fill the time with cooking, exploring the art scene in Houston, taking a day trip to picnic on the beach on Galveston Island, watching movies on Mathias's laptop, and spending hours in a tangle of saliva, sweat, and sheets.

Yoda and Oliver have become fast friends. Sweet little Oliver won't stop following Yoda. If Yoda is standing, Oliver nips at his heels until the two of them start chasing each other, Oliver hurling his teeny, twelve-pound body toward all fifty pounds of Yoda, who gently bites Oliver's scruff and places his paw on his back to show him who is boss. If Yoda lies down, Oliver curls up next to Yoda's belly or lies on Yoda's back. Yoda feigns indifference. But I'm on to him, especially when he looks at me with one sleepy eye open, then closes it, snuggles into Oliver, and lets out a soft sigh as he falls asleep.

Mathias is playful and brings out a lighter, whimsical side of me. Being with him, I don't have to think about the heavy issues, like paying rent on an empty apartment in Santa Monica, finding a job to replenish my depleted bank account, or that Mathias is even more broke than me, and needs a more consistent flow of income than his art brings in. We are not cut from the same cloth, not even close. Of course, I still haven't found shama, and I can't spend the rest of my life driving around the country looking for it, can I? However, blissfully, none of that matters for either of us. Our passion is a welcome escape from the serious adult issues of life that can wait.

Harry who?

One evening, after enjoying another culinary creation at his apartment, Mathias pushes his dinner plate away, rests his forearms on the table, and clasps his hands. "I need to tell you something." He looks down, unable to meet my eyes. "I'm bipolar."

When he says the words, my heart drops through the soles of my feet, and despite trying to hide my concern, it's all over my face. I reach over the table and take his hand in mine.

He continues. "I've struggled a lot with it in the past, and over the years I've learned what works to keep me stable, which is my top priority in life."

"What works for you?" I inquire. He seems balanced now while we talk about it and has appeared stable since we met.

"As long as I run every day and take my medication, I'm fine. I'm committed to doing both because I want a stable life."

I've known several people diagnosed with bipolar disorder, some who take care of themselves and live relatively normal lives, and others who live tortured, painful lives filled with deep, dark demons. In the latter case, the disease can be as hard on the family and loved ones as it is on the individual affected. Yet bipolar is an illness, one that is often treatable. I tell myself that I wouldn't abstain from dating someone just because of a disease like diabetes or asthma, so if Mathias is taking care of his health, then I shouldn't close the door on us.

When the credit card finally arrives a week after I lost it, I invite Mathias and Oliver to go to Louisiana with Yoda and me. Mathias was born in the state and sports a sexy Louisiana drawl with long, lazy vowels. I want to be with him in his home state. Without hesitating, he says yes. So, the next day we load up Princess; Mathias drives, I'm in the passenger seat, and Yoda and Oliver are in the back.

We drive first to his hometown, Lafayette, to spend two nights with his parents. Even though Mathias and I have only recently met, his parents warmly greet Yoda and me. They even join Mathias and me to give Princess a much-needed wash and wax in their driveway. We fill our two days with a swamp boat tour of an alligator-packed bayou, eating copious amounts of crawfish and my first taste of frog legs, and soaking in the backyard Jacuzzi.

After Lafayette, we continue to New Orleans and stay outside the French Quarter. We listen to jazz, share bowls of spicy gumbo, and visit as many dog-friendly places as we can find. The latter is easy with bartenders waving us down to tell us our dogs are welcome.

One morning, Mathias and I stand outside of Café Du Monde waiting to order *café au lait* and *beignets*—those warm, puffy, rectangular-shaped donuts smothered in powdered sugar synonymous with the French Quarter. The irresistible smell of fried dough and chicory coffee fills the air. Yoda, Oliver, and a little terrier in line behind us start playfully biting each other's necks.

"It's a love fest," exclaims Mathias.

The terrier's owner extends her hand to us. "Hi, my name is Mary. Max is so happy to have dogs to play with. He's been going stir crazy since we left home in Minneapolis."

"I'm Mathias, and the pug is my dog, Oliver," says Mathias.

"I'm Kee Kee, and this ball of energy is my dog, Yoda. What are you doing so far from home?"

"Max and I are taking a six-week road trip. We're driving from Minnesota to Florida, making a lot of stops on the way."

"I'm on a road trip, too!" I say. "I left Santa Monica over four months ago."

Mary asks, "What's your final destination?"

Mathias and I look at each other and laugh.

"I have no idea. I lost my job, and I'm not sure what comes next, so I thought maybe I'd find my answers on the road."

"Wow, our stories are similar," Mary exclaims. "I worked with UPS for twenty-five years, and they laid me off, so I also don't know what is next. I'll probably never have the opportunity to take another long road trip, so I'm taking advantage of my severance package to travel. How do you two know each other?"

We reach the front of the line, and Mathias orders for all three of us while I tell Mary the story of meeting through my blog. We take our coffees and beignets to a nearby park bench so the dogs can keep playing.

It's comforting to hear that Mary and her dog are trying to find answers on the road just as Yoda and I are. It reminds me of the guy with the bearded dragon I met at the rest stop in Wyoming, and Brenda, the gourmet popcorn salesperson in Hot Springs, Arkansas. Looking around at the people near us, I wonder how many others recently lost jobs and are trying to find their way?

Talking with Mary is so enjoyable that we agree to meet later for dinner at a dog-friendly restaurant, which, according to Mary, serves the best shrimp *étouffée* in the state.

While in New Orleans, Mathias and I don't do anything too costly, and even make a game out of spending as little money together as possible. We're both counting our pennies as we rebuild our lives, which makes me feel a tighter connection with Mathias. We understand each other.

After we return to Houston, Mathias unexpectedly lands a lucrative new position as a senior staff graphic artist, so his days will soon be filled with the pressures of a new full-time job. I know it's time for Yoda and me to leave. Real life is starting again for him, and it would be selfish of me to stay. However, unlike Mathias, I'm not ready to re-enter my old life. How would I ever prepare for that?

Meanwhile, I can't keep paying rent on an empty, expensive Santa Monica apartment. I never imagined we'd be gone this long, but at this point, I know that I'm not ready to leave life on the road. So, I send an email notice to my landlord that I will move out at the end of March. We'll head back to LA to pack up the apartment, put my belongings in storage, and then continue on the road for at least a few more months.

Mathias walks me to my car the morning we leave. We stand next to Princess, and I hug him long and tight, trying to imprint in my memory his smell, his taste, and the feel of his arms around me. We both know our passionate three-and-a-half-week affair has been a gift we'll treasure forever. Yet his life is in Houston, and mine is on the road for now.

A few miles down the road, tears sting my eyes as they meet Yoda's in the rearview mirror. "Will we ever see Mathias and Oliver again?"

I've been on this road trip long enough for the lesson of the road to become clear as soon as I turn my focus from the rearview mirror to the view through the windshield in front of me: Don't get hung up on the past, and keep looking forward, because something good is always ahead.

TWENTY
San Antonio

*H*e was a gift; it was not meant to last. He was a gift; it was not meant to last. He was a gift; it was not meant to last.

Rinse and repeat. If I say these words in my head enough times as I drive, I hope I'll eventually believe them in my heart. The road presents me with many gifts, and Starr and Mathias are two of my favorites. My experiences with them have made me feel alive, more than I have felt in years.

When I tire of driving and the roads are getting precarious, Yoda and I stop for the night in San Antonio. A freak February winter storm is muscling through Texas, bringing a sloppy mixture of sleet, snow, and freezing rain—my three favorite things.

I'm lucky tonight. I called in a favor to my law school friend, a senior executive with Hyatt Hotels, and snagged a room for free. It's not just any room. It is an executive room on the ninth floor with an expansive view of the River Walk. He even arranged for the manager to leave a fruit plate and bottle of wine in the room. I'm so excited to have a nice hotel room that I do a cartwheel after the bellhop leaves. The room is *that* big.

In the 140 days I've been on the road, I've experienced extraordinary generosity from people offering me guest rooms to crash in. When it comes to hotels, though, the sting of my shrinking bank account has me in the routine of booking basic, no-frills accommodations. So right now, all I can think about is ordering room service, watching a movie, and snuggling with Yoda under the warmth of the plush covers on the king-sized cushion-topped bed in this posh hotel room.

However, before we can settle in, Yoda needs a walk.

It is dusk, and I am the only person braving the freezing temperatures along the famed River Walk. My fingers are numb, my eyelashes frozen, and I can't feel the tip of my nose. It's 17 degrees Fahrenheit with a wind chill below zero, and I don't have warm gloves or thermal socks. I can't imagine it's any more pleasant for Yoda. Despite wearing a fur coat, he walks bare-pawed on wet, frozen pavement, listening to me desperately pleading to hurry up and do his business. It's hardly as if my pleas are going to speed things up.

He languidly looks up with his big, caramel-colored eyes as if to stubbornly declare, "Ma, I've been trapped in the back of your Prius for hours. I'm taking my time."

"Please, Yoda, just go!"

I hop from one grey Chuck Taylor-clad foot to the other in a futile attempt to help the blood circulate through my toes as I curl my hands into fists inside my thinly knit gloves to bring feeling back to my freezing fingers. Finally, he squats.

When I stand after cleaning up after Yoda and spin around to start the mad dash back to the warmth of our hotel, I look up and come face to face with a cowboy. He's tall and lean with short blond hair peeking out from under a black wide-brimmed, high-crowned cowboy hat firmly perched on his head. He wears well-worn scuffed black western cowboy boots, crisp dark denim jeans, and a black quilted down vest over his white dress shirt with a purple cotton turtleneck peeking out of the collar. His cheeks are rosy from the cold, and his friendly brown eyes have a befuddled expression.

"You look lost," I say.

"I'm looking for the Howl at the Moon piano bar and I can't find it," he proclaims in frustration, steam puffing out of his mouth into the cold air.

"Sorry, I don't know where it is."

"I know it's in this block of the River Walk, but I've been wandering back and forth looking for it. Damn, it's cold!" he cries as he rubs his hands together.

He's heading in the same direction as Yoda and me, so we start walking together.

"I'm Kee Kee, and this is Yoda. We're on a road trip and just got into town."

He introduces himself as Wyatt and says he's from Alabama. He tells me he used to be a professional cowboy, but one day he suffered a near fatal injury in the ring. It had something to do with a bull impaling him where it counts. *Ouch.*

"So, with that, my career as a cowboy ended. That's when I hung up my lasso and became a high school biology teacher."

"How does an Alabama high school biology teacher end up in San Antonio during a winter storm?" I ask.

"I'm still a cowboy at heart, so I came for the weekend for the San Antonio Stock Show and Rodeo."

Something is telling me I need to hear Wyatt's full story. So, less than five minutes after we meet, we duck into the Hard Rock Café for hot cocoa. Thank goodness the hostess takes pity on our need to thaw out and lets me hide Yoda under our table, tucked into a private corner of the near-empty room.

As I sit with Wyatt, the cowboy, hugging my warm mug of cocoa to my chest, neither of us can talk fast enough. Our record-setting quick connection is surreal. It's almost as if we look into each other's eyes, see something we recognize, and then start talking over one another to tell our stories. Or maybe it has to do with us being grateful to see another human being out and about in this painfully cold and lonely weather.

Wyatt recently went through his own existential crisis. As he tells me his story, I cling to each of his words.

"After my bull-riding injury, I traded my cowboy boots and denim for khakis and dress shirts, a Mercedes, and world travel. I got so caught up in living the life I thought I was supposed to live that I completely turned my back on my roots," he says. "I mean, I didn't even wear jeans 'cause I thought jeans were part of my cowboy past. But then one day I woke up and couldn't remember the last time I was happy."

Not being true to himself caught up with him. He missed the man he used to be. He missed his inner cowboy. He's worked hard over the last couple of years to find himself again—the real Wyatt. Part of that means breaking out the old cowboy attire and coming to San Antonio for the weekend to enjoy the rodeo. Wyatt sure seems to have found the route to shama.

Maybe the path to shama involves living with a cowgirl vibe? Not Annie Oakley. Not a cowgirl in a ride-a-horse-and-herd-cattle type of way—those women have forged a life of hard physical labor and mental perseverance, bringing skill and courage to their work. I'm talking about cowgirl figuratively. Wouldn't a cowgirl pack up her dog and car and drive out into the wild world by herself? Hells yeah. I've always wished that I could kick up my spurs and bust out of my rut, but I've been too blooming scared of living outside of the box and breaking my restrictive self-imposed life rules. Meanwhile, I'm convinced we all have an inner bohemian, devil-may-care alter ego begging to be unleashed, imploring us to throw caution to the wind, but so many of us go for the safe, known, and ultimately boring choice. *Moi?* Most definitely the latter.

So, instead of embracing my inner cowgirl, I've spent my adulthood following the rules and doing what I've believed others expected me to do with my life. As Starr said, a goody two-shoes. I always want to excel, but damned if I don't feel uneasy if I do stand out from the crowd.

Self to my buried spicy alter ego: *Go where it's safe, Kee Kee. You better not stand out or someone will mock ya and shoot you down.*

I've been afraid to put my twin six-shooters in their holsters and ride bareback on that bucking horse of living life with wide-eyed adventure. Hey there, cowboys; how's that for a visceral metaphor?

Wyatt stirs the mini marshmallows in his cup of steaming hot chocolate while he talks. He's the most recent of my many new road friends who've all shown me that I am not alone in my searching and questioning.

One thing, for sure: This journey of self-discovery is quite a ride, and whatever the Universe shows me, I will not waste it. My pain torments me so much that I wallow in it instead of realizing a purpose behind the angst. This wannabe cowgirl feels the Wild West of life guiding her through the desert to cool, still waters. She's ready to drink. *I'm suddenly full of metaphors.*

I smile at this latest lesson of the road: It is time to embrace my inner cowgirl and become the woman I am meant to be.

TWENTY-ONE

Ozona and Las Cruces

Damn if my recent thought-swirls aren't nine times out of ten about men. Leaving San Antonio after two nights, my head spins thinking about Harry, Wyatt the Cowboy, and Mathias, whom I haven't heard from since I left Houston.

Harry sent an intriguing email last night that said, "Been thinking about you a lot recently. How are you doing, and where in the country are you? Would love to connect again sometime. I travel a lot on business, so maybe we'll be in the same city at the same time?"

I'm having trouble reading between the lines. Is Harry seeking an invitation? Or was it an offhand comment? With Mathias on the brain, my heart struggles to interpret any subtext of Harry's reaching out. I respond noncommittally. "I'm heading out of the Lone Star State, finally making my way toward the Golden State. Should be back soon."

I'm disappointed that Mathias hasn't called, even though we agreed that, despite our immediate connection, it's impossible to make something work due to our circumstances. Although we emailed daily for a few weeks before we met, the stark reality is that we've spent only about three weeks together. I have little right to feel hurt that he shut the door on us the moment I left because of the unspoken assumption between us that ours was an in-the-moment fling and nothing more. Neither of us made any promises to the other. But still, it hurts. A lot.

So, driving west on I-10, my thoughts shift to my conversation with Wyatt and how I want to embrace the cowgirl spirit to live with shama. What would a cowgirl do in this situation? She would buckle down, move on from Mathias, stop trying to tame the bucking broncos, and enjoy the Wild West of the present moment, which means I am finally going to Marfa!

During this entire trip, I've had my heart set on visiting a tiny little artist haven named Marfa in the high desert of West Texas—part of the Wild West. With more art galleries than people, it's famous for the Marfa Lights, an alleged paranormal phenomenon that supposedly can be seen in the sky on clear nights. Of course, during almost five months on the road, I have repeatedly made road trip plans, only to have them change nearly every time.

When itineraries have fallen through, things have always worked out for the better. I've made new friends I wouldn't have met if I'd followed my plan. I've visited some new favorite little towns I wouldn't have seen and had some of the most magical experiences of my life that wouldn't have happened had I stuck to my plan. So, you'd think by now that I wouldn't cling too tightly to any given itinerary. But this is Marfa, and I so very much want to go.

A light snow begins to fall a few hours into my drive, but I ignore my fear of driving in the snow and plan to press on through to Marfa. Then the freezing rain starts, which is most definitely something I can't power through. I need to stop. The closest town is Ozona, Texas, a small town somewhere in the vast barren region between San Antonio and El Paso. Luckily, I find a dog-friendly motel with a room.

When I check in, I ask the front desk clerk what there is to do in town.

She pauses, purses her lips, and looks at the ceiling while she thinks about it. "Well, we have a Dollar General. There's also a gift shop at the truck stop seven miles east of here on I-10." She makes a sniffing noise and rubs her nose. "I wish we had a Salvation Army because it would be fun to shop for thrift items."

I plan to get up early and continue to Marfa, but I wake up to Princess covered in snow and news that sections of the freeway are closed due to snow and ice. Stuck in Ozona for a second night, I call our hotel in Marfa to attempt to push our reservation a night, only to learn it is fully booked for the next two nights. I reluctantly cancel our Marfa trip because I refuse to spend a single night longer in Ozona. I'm sure it's lovely for the Ozonians, but I had my heart set on something else, and the town hasn't laid out the welcome mat for me.

It starts with my dilapidated motel room. The carpet is stained, the bathroom light doesn't work, the TV is broken, and the piece of tin built into the wall that is supposed to be a heater loudly clanks its little heart out while it tries to churn out a bit of heat. The worst part? The toilet can't handle toilet paper, so I must put it in the trash can next to the loo. *Say what?* I've traveled enough in third-world countries to be fairly comfortable with this practice, but I never expected to encounter it in a U.S. hotel for seventy-nine dollars plus a ten-dollar pet fee.

Determined to make lemonade out of sour lemons, I bundle up and take Yoda for a walk around the frozen town center in the arctic chill. It's small, so this takes all of ten minutes. We see a frozen tiered fountain with icicles and frozen blobs sticking out every which way. It looks like a beautiful abstract ice sculpture. Hyped on a giant sign in the middle of the town square, I'm hoping to discover why Ozona calls itself "The Biggest Little Town in the World." However, I only find a large statue of Davy Crockett on our walk. I take a photo and set off to unearth the connection between Ozona and Davy Crockett. It turns out there is none. A city worker tells me the statue is here because someone donated it to the park.

Ironically, the one building of interest is the Crockett County Museum. A sweet elderly woman who runs the place greets me and seems excited to see a visitor. In broken English, she asks for a two-dollar donation, which I happily turn over. Then she tells me to give her a minute as she shuffles off to switch the lights on and turn on the heat. The Museum of Science and Industry, it is not.

The museum features an antique permanent curl machine that resembles a torture device for Medusa—I've never seen anything like it—and two glass display cases filled with slippers, a nod to the slipper manufacturer that used to be in the basement of this building. Strangely, there's a single set of false teeth on display with no explanation. A sign on a wheelbarrow full of sand invites people to dig through to find "genuine" Indian arrowheads (stamped with "Hecho en Mexico"). All in all, the museum does provide an hour's worth of entertainment.

Giving up on finding anything else to do in town, I head back to my hotel room. I love small towns, but my problem with Ozona is how it pretends to be something bigger than it is. Of course, the crazy ice storm has tainted my road trip experience here, which I'm pretty sure means I'm not experiencing the Ozona that many of its residents love and call home. Regardless, I can't find the positive spin or the lesson of the road with this one, except that the weather is the great disrupter of plans.

The minute the ice melts and the I-10 freeway opens, I head to the city of Las Cruces in New Mexico, aka the Land of Enchantment. I hadn't intended to go, but since Marfa is no longer on my route, I must land somewhere for the night.

I stay at an inexpensive and delightfully artsy boutique hotel in Las Cruces with California king beds and a blissful maze of gardens in the courtyard filled with chile pepper plants. The hotel's new owners are a lovely couple from Phoenix who purchased it last year. When I check in, they show me their blueprint for building the world's largest chile pepper in front of the hotel later this year—forty-seven feet long and constructed out of more than two tons of concrete. When they learn we have driven almost seven hours without stopping for lunch, they deliver chips and salsa, green tea, tiramisu, and a dog treat to our room. I know now that the Ozona lemons made my lemonade.

Before climbing into bed, I check my email. Harry responded to my reply to his email. What I find quite curious is that my heart doesn't get the usual zoomies when I see his name in my mailbox. It also doesn't break into a flat-out gallop from a standing start when I read again that Harry wants to see me when I return. I send a short email telling him I should be in LA within the next few weeks. I suggest we have coffee when I get back.

I'm nonchalant as I type, almost as if I'm writing to a distant acquaintance and not a former lover who has had an ironclad grip on my heart for nearly a decade. My heart has been on the move. Our timing is always off. Over the years, when one of us reaches out, the other is in a committed relationship. Since breaking up, we've never been single at the same time. Right now, I'm still smitten with Mathias. Oh yeah, there's also the small (totally *not* small) issue of Harry being married.

In any event, when writing my essays for Starr, I began to wonder if I've given Harry too much power over me and my life, power he didn't even know he had. Have I been using my disjointed memory of us together as an excuse to avoid lasting intimacy with any other man? I start to feel queasy about who I've been over the years: a woman prevented from fully living life in the moment by suffocating herself with indiscriminate memories of the past.

Since I've hit it off with the wife of the husband-wife duo hotel owners, her husband stays behind to run the hotel's front desk while the two of us go to breakfast at a nearby French bakery.

We sit at a window table with a view of my car parked on the street. Yoda has jumped to the driver's seat and is staring at us from behind the steering wheel. It makes us laugh.

"I love that you're driving around the country trying to create a new life for yourself," she gushes.

"I'm a work in progress and have a long way to go," I say with a sigh. "But you inspire me so much. I'm curious how you and your husband decided to remake your lives completely."

She takes a bite of her croissant and then dabs the corners of her mouth with her napkin. "We weren't happy with our careers and wanted to be our own bosses. We found this hotel for sale a couple of years ago, so we bought it, moved from Phoenix to Las Cruces, and started renovating."

"You did such a nice job. Clearly a lot of love went into every part of the place."

"It's been hard physical labor and somewhat emotional, but we're both passionate about this work and are grateful we can do it together. Once we get the concrete chile pepper built out front, we'll take a breather from the constant home improvements."

Contentment shines clearly through her eyes as she speaks. If she hasn't discovered it already, she seems to be on her way to finding shama.

After breakfast, Yoda and I head to the historic village of Old Mesilla. Within ten minutes of wandering around the main plaza, I meet a man named Carlo, an Emmy-winning documentary filmmaker who calls Mesilla home. It is wild to meet someone from my former industry who lives in this tiny town and shares my name. That's because Carlo's nickname is Kiki. So, Kiki proceeds to act as Kee Kee's tour guide for the next couple of hours, giving me an insider's perspective of Old Mesilla.

Carlo tells me that in 1854, the United States purchased the Mexican village of Mesilla to resolve a long-standing border dispute in the Mexican-American War. Mesilla became an important stop on the Butterfield stagecoach route and, in the 1880s, became a lively social center. Sealing its importance as a prominent player in the Wild Wild West, in 1881, authorities tried Billy the Kid and sentenced him to hang at the jail and courthouse located on the main plaza. The jail is still there, except now it is a gift shop. Another example of commercial "progress" in the form of corporate creep blanketing the historic character of a place. At least it's not a big box store.

Part of the charm of Old Mesilla is how it retains the look and feel of an old Mexican border town. Most of the buildings surrounding the main plaza are traditional adobe structures that serve as a reminder of the town's significant history. Today the Mesilla Plaza is home to the Basilica of San Albino, unique shops, art galleries, pottery shops, and many eateries and wine bars.

Every Sunday, Mesilla Plaza hosts the local Farmers and Crafts Market. Carlo and I make plans to meet for dinner in an hour, and then Yoda and I wander around the market. Here, I meet an older man named Don at his booth, whose grandfather was born behind the Basilica when Mesilla was still part of Mexico. Today, Don runs his multi-generational family farm and sells salsas and flame-roasted green chiles. After sampling each, I leave with two jars of the good stuff and rush off to meet Carlo at a small restaurant off the main square.

We sit on the outdoor patio with Yoda lying at our feet, and I devour the best chiles rellenos I've ever had, followed by my first ever Mexican Coke. I'm not usually a soda drinker. However, I'm convinced I'll forever salivate when I remember combining this Mexican Coke with the scrumptious meal. Carlo is friends with the owner of the restaurant, who brings us complimentary glasses of horchata, a chilled, creamy rice drink with hints of cinnamon and vanilla. It's another first for me.

Before returning to our hotel in Las Cruces, Yoda and I walk Carlo a few blocks to the little century-old adobe where he lives. He lets me hold his Emmy and shows me photos of his family. I leave his home smiling, telling Yoda, "We are so lucky to keep making all these new friends everywhere we go."

New Mexico is turning into such an enchanted experience that I stay a second night. The next morning, Yoda and I drive to White Sands National Monument, the world's largest gypsum dune field. The white dunes rise up to sixty feet high and cover 275 square miles. We spend hours hiking over the wave-like dunes. It is like nothing I've ever seen. White rippled mounds of silky sand for as far as my eyes can see. There's snow on some of the mounds, and kids have brought sleds to slide down. Yoda and I sit on a high sandy peak. He leans into me, and I wrap my arm around him and smile when the kids start making combo sand-snow angels.

Later, as we settle into our cozy hotel room, I reflect that if Ozona hadn't been such a perfectly awful experience, I wouldn't have discovered Las Cruces. Herein is the latest lesson of the road: the lemonade will always be there when I have the patience to squeeze out the juice. How many times will I need to learn this lesson before it sticks? Without fail, it has been true on this road trip. Looking back on my life—well, after each difficult spell, the lemonade was eventually served there, too.

TWENTY-TWO

Bisbee, Bowie, and Safford

As much as I've enjoyed my brief stay in New Mexico, my heart remains heavy. I'm not ready to face Los Angeles. I've still not heard from Mathias. As I drive, I ask, "How did I ever think I could find answers on the road?"

Good ol' self-doubt, showing up right on schedule.

Yes, I have had some incredible experiences, so why do I feel as if I'm returning to my old life, even though my sole reason is to pack up my apartment, put my belongings in storage, and continue on the road?

My friend Dawn calls in the nick of time to keep me from spiraling.

I lament to her, "It's pretty humbling to think that I've spent so many months on the road searching for answers, but I'm returning to LA without any."

"I'm pretty sure you have more insights than you realize," Dawn replies.

In addition to being a world-class matchmaker (she introduced me first to Harry and then the cheating boyfriend, which led to me adopting Yoda), Dawn is a friend who consistently offers sage life advice.

"I've been gone so long that I wonder what has changed in Los Angeles."

"Kee Kee, LA hasn't changed. The only thing that's changed is you."

Have I?

I've arrived in Bisbee, Arizona, a funky artists' haven nestled a mile high on the hillside of a mountain. During my months driving aimlessly yet purposefully around the country, I've done my best to create new daily experiences, which means traveling to places I've never been and avoiding areas where I spent time in the past. I've heard that mentally stimulating activities boost brainpower and help keep our brains sharp as we age. For example, learning a new language or driving alternate routes to work forge new neural pathways in the brain. Applying this theory to my life on the road, by challenging myself each day with fresh experiences, I'll kick-start a new way of thinking and figure out how to live with shama. *C'mon, neural pathways, forge ahead.*

All said, Bisbee is a place I briefly visited a couple of years ago on a birthday trip with some friends. I've wanted to return to explore some of the town's old-world charm and new-world personality. It's an old copper mining town in southeastern Arizona's Mule Mountains about ninety miles southeast of Tucson. Bisbee's Historic District, a Registered National Historic Landmark, has a European feel with its hilly terrain and steep, narrow streets. Many of the mountain colony's eclectic Victorian bungalows can only be reached by trekking up deteriorating stairways built into the picturesque mountainside.

We stay for a few days in Bisbee, and I visit galleries, artist studios, coffee shops, and the old copper mine. Although I don't encounter any ghosts in this allegedly haunted town, the visit is gifting me a handful of new memories with Yoda and a mental recharge that leaves me feeling more alive than when I arrived.

That electric feeling may be because I finally hear from Mathias. He calls on my second night here and I pick up on the first ring.

His first words are, "I miss you, Kee Kee."

I melt.

And then, "Move to Houston and be with me."

I panic.

"Oh, Mathias, I miss you too. But moving to Texas isn't something that has ever remotely been on my radar."

"I'd love to move to LA," he says, "but I know you no longer want to live there."

Besides, he has a new job in Houston with a fat paycheck, and I'm still unemployed.

"We have something special, Kee Kee. We need to explore it."

I ask him to let me think about it.

It's my final morning in Bisbee, and the innkeeper of our B&B serves me a beautiful asparagus frittata, and then sits down across the table with her cup of tea. She's a grandmotherly type with whom I'm immediately comfortable. Over a homemade gourmet breakfast and bottomless cups of coffee, I tell her about Mathias, his idea of me moving to Houston, and how I rarely take risks when making major decisions.

She smiles as if she is about to let me in on a big secret. "Honey, the way to happiness in life is not dwelling on *what ifs* but taking action."

I look at her, considering her words.

"What do you have to lose?" she questions. "If it doesn't work out, you will not have a *what if*; instead, you'll have another adventure under your belt."

After packing up Princess, I hug the innkeeper. "Thank you for sharing your wisdom. You've given me a lot to think about."

Yoda and I leave Bisbee and head east, backtracking a couple of hours. We're headed toward what I hope will be an overnight adventure. A few days ago, I was driving through the parched Arizona desert on my way to Bisbee. Having seen no sign of human life for miles, I spotted a lone billboard for a Shell gas station that touts it is home to Dwayne's Fresh Jerky, a store that sells jerky, gourmet olives, honey, and nuts. When driving long stretches between towns, I always fill up with gas whenever I have the opportunity because I don't want to risk running out of gas by myself in an area with no cell reception. The gas station and the possibility of snacking on some olives and nuts (with beef jerky for Yoda) made it a no-brainer that I would stop.

After I filled Princess Leia with gas and walked Yoda around the parking lot, I started talking with the owner of Dwayne's Fresh Jerky. It turns out Dwayne is also from Southern California. One of the nice things about connecting with strangers on the road is that I often discover local gold nuggets that never make the travel guides. That's exactly what happened during my conversation with Dwayne. He mentioned a nearby remote RV park that is home each February to a group of seventy- and eighty-year-old former Western Swing Hall of Famers. For the past twenty-seven years, these seniors have annually road-tripped from all over the U.S. to gather in the Arizona desert for a month-long musical jam. They call their gathering "Sideman Jamboree," because many have had enviable careers touring as sidemen and women with some of the world's greatest country music stars. Decades ago, they decided that each February is their turn to take center stage.

My cheeks flushed, my jaw dropped, and I begged him to take me to them. Lucky for me, he agreed. He asked his wife to run the jerky counter, and I followed Dwayne's car. He took me straight to a woman named Judy Hall, who, along with her husband John, has owned this Bowie, Arizona, RV park on "Music Road" since 1982. They live in Alaska in the summer but call the RV park home during the winter months. Judy's illustrious music career started at the age of fourteen. She has toured with musical artists Sara Vaughan, Ernest Tubb, Merle Haggard, Waylon Jennings, George Strait, Jimmy Buffett, and Tennessee Ernie Ford. Judy and her husband became homesteaders in Alaska about fifty years ago. Because they didn't have a phone, Judy never quite knew when she was going to be needed; she kept a suitcase packed so that she was ready whenever a helicopter came to pick her up for the next leg of each tour. Without warning, of course.

After meeting Judy, I desperately wanted to hear the nightly jamboree that takes place in a barn they built on the property. Judy invited me to come back after my visit in Bisbee, and her young friend, Shane, a former Alaska State Trooper in his late thirties, had kindly offered to let me and Yoda stay the night in his empty spare camper. That's why we left Bisbee and are now driving back to the RV park.

Road-tripping has taught me to love freeway rest stops. Stopping at one is a triple bonanza: (1) the obvious potty break, and possible coffee refill if the vending machines cooperate; (2) a much-needed walk and water break for Yoda; and (3) an opportunity to have a conversation with someone other than Yoda and Princess Leia.

Some state rest stops on this trip have been better than others. The Pacific Northwest had the friendliest rest stops, offering free coffee, wild blackberries for the picking, and well-groomed hiking trails. Missouri had the most whimsical rest stops on Route 66, guaranteed to win a smile from even the crankiest traveler. I was hard-pressed to find any rest stops at all in Texas. However, there were plenty of "picnic areas" off the freeway, without bathrooms and often littered with trash. Arizona recently began reopening some of the thirteen rest stops it closed last year due to a budget crunch. On the drive to the RV park, at one of these recently reopened rest stops in Arizona's otherworldly Texas Canyon, I meet two likeable lanky guys named Will and Brian.

Initially, I don't notice them, because I am exploring the gigantic weathered granite boulders strewn everywhere and watching out for the "poisonous snakes and insects" warned about on the posted signs. Then, Will calls out to Yoda. If Yoda takes a liking to someone, then so do I. Yoda likes Will and Brian. They are traveling from California in a red Honda with Alaska plates. As most rest-stop conversations go, our talk inevitably turns into "Where are you headed?" They are driving to a hot springs campground called Essence of Tranquility in Safford, Arizona, about an hour from the rest stop.

More hot springs? Yes, please. In addition to rejuvenating my soul, a hot soak might be the only thing that will help relieve the spasm in my right hip, which is sorely out of joint from all my driving. I jot down directions and tell Will and Brian I'll search for the place on my drive back from the desert RV park.

When Yoda and I arrive at the RV park in the late afternoon, a biting cold wind is already whipping up. Shane welcomes us and shows me the camper that Yoda and I will call home for the night and how to work the little desktop space heater. Then, he invites us into his RV for a pre-dinner cocktail, something we sneak in in private because most seniors here don't drink. We toast to new friends and fun adventures, then the three of us head to the barn for dinner.

At 5 p.m. each night, all the musicians and their spouses gather in the barn for a potluck dinner. They each bring a dish with the food and supplies they brought into the desert, since the only store for miles around is the nearby Shell station. The buffet table features all the classic recipes you'd find at a church potluck: chicken tater casserole, ravioli lasagna, coleslaw, baked beans, sweet potato chili, deviled eggs, strawberry pretzel salad, seven-layer salad, and a dessert table with everything from peanut butter pie to carrot cake. I bring only my smile, my dog, and a camera, which are good enough for everyone to generously feed me with their homemade dishes until I'm so stuffed that I fear I won't be able to roll myself to my camper at the end of the night.

After dinner, Sideman Jamboree begins. The barn's walls are decorated with moose taxidermy mounts, cowboy gear, and musical instruments hanging every which way. Rows of state flags and even a few international flags are strung high above our heads to represent all the states and countries of people who have attended Sideman Jamboree over the years. Behind an area cleared for dancing in front of the stage are lines of folding chairs. A sign next to the cleared area reads *No Spurs on Dance Floor*. Behind the stage, under a gigantic American Flag, is a huge banner that reads *SIDEMAN JAMBOREE #27* for the twenty-seventh year of this wonderful, secret musical celebration.

As the music begins, Shane plunks a cowboy hat on my head, and I automatically slap my knee to the rhythm. They promised me a show, and I'm given one. Fifty to sixty of these senior citizens, decked out in their stage clothes, have the energy of people a third their age. They play western swing, traditional country, big band, jazz, blues, and even a little rock. It's a rare song where Judy isn't on stage singing. She's wearing tight denim jeans, a denim vest with red, white, and blue stars embroidered on it, and a white shirt underneath with matching stars embossed on the front. One of the men on stage starts playing the steel guitar, Judy sings "yee haw!" into the microphone, and the drummer, two guitarists, and a bass player join in. She wiggles her hips and stomps her boot in time with the music, then looks down at me and winks as she breaks out singing "Swinging Doors."

The music and dancing continue for almost three hours, after which I crank the space heater in the camper and snuggle up with Yoda in my down sleeping bag. I don't sleep very well—I'm cold, and my mind chatters in overdrive about encountering this music festival in the middle of nowhere. And there's Mathias. Should I say yes? Should I move to Texas? What would it be like to wake up with him every morning?

I say my goodbyes and get an early start, swinging by the Shell station for coffee and yogurt, and to say goodbye to Dwayne, who is already working at Dwayne's Fresh Jerky. Then I head toward Tucson for the night. But first, I have a pit stop to make.

The directions Will and Brian gave me to the hot springs campground are cryptic, my GPS doesn't recognize the address, and I can't find the highway signage. With the help of a gas station attendant, I finally find the place, which is quiet. The first people I encounter are my rest-stop comrades. Will and Brian seem surprised to see me, but are so hospitable that Brian gives up his favorite hot mineral spring tub for me to soak in.

The hot spring community is intriguing. While I've visited beautiful luxury hot spring spas in Palm Springs, Napa Valley,

San Luis Obispo, New Mexico, Montecatini Terme in Italy, Bath in England, and the mountains outside of Tokyo, I much prefer a crunchier granola vibe—which is a good thing, because most hot mineral springs are in a run-down state.

Essence of Tranquility is no different. Its website even offers the following caveat:

THIS PLACE IS OUT IN THE DESERT, IN THE COUNTRY, IT IS NOT A CITY, GLITZY DAY SPA, AS SUCH IF THAT IS WHAT YOU ARE WANTING THIS IS NOT THE PLACE FOR YOU. IT IS A SMALL AREA WITH SOME GRASS, A FEW TREES AND PAPYRUS PLANTS. IT'S REALLY NOT TO (sic) BAD.

The website is right; it isn't too bad—it's fantastic. Each hot mineral spring tub offers a different theme and temperature and has a latch on the door for private soaks. My tub features a big Buddha statue serving as a reminder that the purpose of my road trip is to *seek shama.* I soak in 104-degree Fahrenheit water in private for an entire hour for a mere five dollars. If I hadn't made plans to stay tonight in Tucson with friends of a friend, I would rent one of the simple casitas in the adjoining campground and stare longingly at the treatment rooms. Being a road trip cowgirl with no salary, I've learned to forgo indulging myself in luxuries such as massages and pedicures.

When I leave the hot springs, my hip pain is a bit milder than when I arrived, and my most recent lesson of the road has been right in front of me this entire trip: *talk to people.* The new friends I've made on the road have shown me I'm not alone in my journey to find shama, and many conversations have also led me to some pretty awesome off-the-beaten-path road trip discoveries. On this leg of my trip, Dwayne from Dwayne's Fresh Jerky led me to the Sideman Jamboree RV Park, and Will and Brian led me to the little slice of desert hot spring heaven. Most importantly, as I drive toward Tucson, reflecting on my conversation with the innkeeper of the B&B in Bisbee, I finally make a decision.

I look at Yoda in the rearview mirror and proclaim, "Yoda, we're moving to Houston to live happily ever after."

TWENTY-THREE
The Grand Canyon and Tecopa Springs

It is time for me to face Los Angeles. For the five months I've been on the road with Yoda, my apartment has been sitting empty. I've been planning on returning to pack up my home and put my belongings in storage to free up that expense and continue on the road. However, I now need to pack up my apartment for another reason: to move across the country. I haven't told anyone about "The Decision" except Yoda and Princess, and, as of last night, Mathias.

"Mathias?" My voice sounds new, about to say something unfamiliar. "The answer is yes!"

"Kee Kee, that is fantastic news! I'm going to rent a place for us to have a fresh start together. Let's figure out the timing for me to come to LA and help you with the move."

The Decision is the biggest I have ever reached without input from others, and I'm taking my time to process the magnitude of what I'm about to do.

With this momentous time on my mind, I find myself in tiny Williams, Arizona, which promotes itself as the "Gateway to the Grand Canyon." Indeed, it's one of the closest cities to the South Rim. After splurging for a twenty-five-dollar day pass, Yoda and I spend four hours walking around the Rim. Peering down at the colorful stratified layers of the canyon, I'm utterly transfixed. As I look into the awe-inspiring natural beauty of the Grand Canyon, it seems as if I'm about to dive into the soul of the Universe. I hide under my baseball cap and behind sunglasses, with tears streaming down my cheeks. The waterworks in the early weeks of my road trip were a healing purge, limited to private time behind the wheel of Princess. Those tears dried up as my road trip progressed; they're not tears of despair this time.

The reasons for my Grand Canyon tears are twofold. First, I am not ready to return to LA, let alone pack up my place. LA has been at the root of all my conflicted feelings about what I'm doing and where I'm going with my life. It was easier to be on this road trip for the last few months, not examining this stuff. It will be staring me in the face back in LA, though. I'm not entirely certain I've found the shama necessary to give me the strength to return and confront what I still see as the failure of my life in LA.

The second reason for my tears comes from the emotional jumble surrounding my plan to move. My usual pattern with decision-making is to fret and analyze the issue from every angle. Will people judge me? Who will agree? Who will disagree? Is my choice responsible? I don't make it if my decision doesn't pass every litmus test possible. From being on the road, I've learned that *no one cares*. Everyone is too busy living their own life to criticize mine. Wyatt the cowboy was right about what's important. I want to live with the cowgirl spirit. A cowgirl would not live in fear of being judged. She would grab life by the reins and yippee-ki-yay into the Texas sunset with her new man.

Right. "I'm not afraid!" I declare, standing at the edge of a 7,000-foot cliff.

I wake up in a Williams motel, looking forward to spending a few days with my friend Chuck at his home in Las Vegas. It's been the plan for months that Yoda and I would visit before we return to

California. Now it seems extra important to spend time with him because I'm excited to tell him about The Decision. But when Chuck calls at the last minute to cancel due to a family emergency, I'm on my own with my decision to pack up and move in with Mathias.

Checkout is in forty minutes, and I need to figure out where to go next. Sitting at my computer, I quickly type "hot springs near Las Vegas." There's one in California called Tecopa Hot Springs. In a rush, I don't research the place or know how to get there. I call them and book a room for tonight.

I plug the address into the GPS for Princess and start a five-hour drive. After a few hours of driving, we cross the California border. It's been five months since I've been on California soil. At the sight of the *WELCOME TO CALIFORNIA* freeway sign, a rush of uncertainty bubbles to the surface. *Why, hello there, self-doubt, my old frenemy.* Has this road trip been a complete bust? Uh-oh, here comes the pile-on. After five months on the road, maybe I've taken a few steps toward shama, but am I strong enough to face Los Angeles?

The "I Welcome Change" sticky note catches my eye. If this journey has been a spiritual bust, what was this road trip all about? Was it about finding a man and moving across the country? Where's my inner peace, my shama? Or maybe Dawn is right, and I have changed, but I'm not seeing the changes? Not yet.

Shaking myself out of autopilot, I see we're in the middle of the Mojave Desert, heading into Death Valley with only one bar left on my gas gauge and no cell reception. For the next hour, I drive as fuel-efficiently as I can. I'm not sure about the real formula for fuel-efficient driving, but my version involves turning off the music and A/C, rolling down the windows, and driving slowly and steadily while holding my breath. The breath-holding likely does it, because I finally land at a gas station with one thirsty car. That'll teach me for breaking my rule to fill the gas tank as soon as Princess's gauge goes below half.

We eventually arrive at Tecopa Hot Springs, a pleasant, unpretentious place with loads of colorful pottery on the grounds and well-loved rustic cabins described on their website as "camping with four walls." If hot springs are involved, gimme clean sheets and a friendly property manager, and I'm in.

After purchasing some art made from license plates a local artist found in the desert, I take a slow, meditative walk with Yoda around Tecopa Hot Springs' forty-foot-long stone labyrinth. Named the Yaga Labyrinth to honor the indigenous Paiute tribe, which discovered the sacred waters centuries ago, it is on a hill overlooking a dry ancient glacial lake bed and the surrounding desert mountains. A kaleidoscope of colors lights up the scene like a kiss from the sunset. With each step, I silently repeat the words *seek shama*. Yoda seems as content as I am and stays at my heel during every turn of the labyrinth. We arrive at the center to a small pile of objects left by people as prayers or symbolic acts of letting go. I take a pen and a business card out of my bag and print the words *Seek Shama*, then tuck the paper into the center of the pile so it doesn't blow away. A deeply sacred act. In a very funky place.

Afterward, while soaking in the hot spring, a tremendous sense of peace, contentment, *and* a new understanding sweep over me. The symbolism of my visit to Tecopa Hot Springs proves to me that I am exactly where I need to be now.

Okay, good start.

Ending up in Death Valley symbolizes the slow death of the tightly wound-up, depressed woman I was when I first embarked on my road trip. The hot spring symbolizes renewal and the birth of the cowgirl I'm becoming.

The more I think about it, the more I like where this story is going.

The labyrinth symbolizes shama, and it occurs to me that I've been experiencing increasing moments of inner peace during the last couple of months.

Go on.

The license plate art I purchased in the gift shop is created from plates from states we have visited and spells out "Jah Love," which I interpret as Universal Love, or God's Love. After all the tears and uncertainty with this road trip, it's as if Jah has been watching over me, making sure I suffer just enough and learn that what I am experiencing is exactly what I need.

The weird thing is that during the past five months on the road, through the hours of crying, soul searching, and trying to find myself, I fell in love (or at least in deep like). Mathias has swept me off my feet, and I'm stoked about The Decision. I am ready to face LA and tell friends and family that I am moving to Houston. Bring it on.

The cowgirl jumps off the fence.

Although much of my positive mindset is about the excitement of moving in with Mathias, it's more than that. Maybe this page-turning, life-shifting, straightaway home stretch is where this journey has been leading me. I'm not saying all my troubles are over, or that paradise is around the corner, but the process of finding shama is starting to make sense to me: searching for inner peace is a lifelong quest. The trick is learning to trust that the road will always be underfoot with each new step I take, or each new mile I drive. Dare I say, I think this moment is the end of something big, and the beginning of something bigger.

Says the cowgirl as she dodges another cow pie.

TWENTY-FOUR
Los Angeles

Life hinges on moments, like meeting Harry for coffee a week after returning to Los Angeles. I'm surprised how emotional I am about saying goodbye to LA, my home of fifteen years, even though I know it hasn't been a healthy home for me. Still, it's home, and I will miss things, like Harry. He chose a charming place in Venice Beach called Rose Café, which is dog-friendly, so I bring Yoda. The anticipation of seeing him unleashes a swarm of butterflies, giving me hiccups and tummy flutters.

Harry is my past; Mathias is my present—a new mantra repeats in my head as I hand the valet my keys. Harry is already sitting at a table on the patio. An intoxicating sizzle of attraction zips up my spine. I tuck some flyaway hair behind my ear and thrust my shoulders back as I walk toward him.

Harry crouches down to greet Yoda, who whines an excited yodel as he puts his front paws on Harry's knees, so his mouth is close enough to lick Harry's cheek. It's the first time they've met, yet it's like watching a reunion between two old friends. It's bittersweet. Harry and I talked about getting a dog together and even installed a doggie door in our home. But the dog never happened, like getting married or having children never happened. While I will always and forever cherish our years together, those years are past. So, before he can say what, if anything, has been on his mind all these months since we last saw one another, I plunge right into the news of my move to Texas.

"I've met someone. His name is Mathias. I'm excited to explore things with him, so I'm taking a leap of faith and moving to Houston in two weeks."

"Oh, wow." His eyes cast downward, as if he's searching for something in his cup of coffee.

"Harry, I think all these years I've put my future on hold because I was subconsciously holding too tight to memories of the past." I'm babbling, not giving him a chance to say anything. I feel a sense of urgency to put it all out on the table before I lose my courage.

Harry is quiet.

"You were my first love, and I think since we broke up, deep down I've been afraid to fully embrace what I had in the moment out of fear of letting go of my magical memories with you. Five months on the road taught me that it's time to move on, and part of that is leaving Los Angeles."

Harry nods as he rubs the back of his neck. The inner ends of his eyebrows raise and pull together as he sips his coffee.

Is he going to say anything?

Harry's Adam's apple moves up as he swallows. "I'm happy for you." He clears his throat. "My wife and I are working on our marriage. We've been seeing a therapist. We want to make it work for the kids."

Yoda leans into my leg and meets my eyes as he rests his head on my thigh. A feeling of security sweeps over me as I hand my empty cup to a passing waiter.

Harry walks us to my car. We hug tightly—that magnetic melding into one another that I've longed for, for years. My mouth is dry, and my throat is tight.

As Yoda and I drive away, Harry is in the rearview mirror, standing beside his car, watching. *Harry is my past; Mathias is my present.*

I blink back tears that threaten to spill over. He never did say why he wanted to meet.

I'm filled with the stark reality of unspoken words, regret, lingering questions, and above all else, a hope for a better future by finally putting this relationship behind me and moving forward with another.

I sit on the floor of my Santa Monica apartment, surrounded by moving boxes half-filled with dishes in bubble wrap, reflecting on six months ago when I proclaimed my need for a new direction. I prayed to find shama: *Help me find my way in this chaotic world and bring me inner peace.*

On the first day of my road trip (which seems a lifetime ago), having no idea where I was going (emotionally or geographically), I blubbered snotty tears all over my steering wheel as I drove up the California coast in the pouring rain. I spent the following five months driving around the United States with my hand-printed words "I Welcome Change" on that decade-old sticky note plastered to my dashboard with duct tape. "I Welcome Change" became my mantra, my friend, my muse.

The Universe eventually listened, and now that it's bringing me change, I welcome it with open arms. Kinda. Sorta. Okay, fine. I'm pushing it away at the same time as I'm desperate to reel it in. Change, no matter how healthy and welcome it may be, takes me out of my comfort zone, which can be painful.

Two days before I move to Texas to live with Mathias, he flies into LA a day ahead of my parents so the four of us can drive Princess and a U-Haul truck to Houston together.

When I pick Mathias up at LAX, our reunion features red flags flying at full mast—a new level of concern, after I've ignored them from the beginning. I'm apprehensive.

DEFCON 4. Above normal readiness; strengthened security measures.

He's a great sport as I drag him to my going-away party in Venice to meet about fifty of my LA friends for cocktails and sunset beach views at the rooftop bar of the Erwin Hotel. I spent fifteen years building this community of friends, and it will be difficult to leave them. My friends support my move to Houston and are incredibly welcoming to Mathias. So far, it's going smoothly.

The friend thing, well, that's the latest lesson of the road. Life is richer with the love and support of friends. During my road trip, in my new role as authentic me, I made many new friends around the country and strengthened old friendships, while wearing my heart on my sleeve. I let people know the reasons for my road trip—that I was lost and in pain. Instead of rejecting me, the old and the new wrapped their arms around me and let me know I would be okay.

Perhaps the excitement of meeting my parents and friends, or our impulsive decision to move in together, starts Mathias on what he calls a "bipolar manic tear," which means he's talking non-stop while quickly changing the topic mid-sentence and constantly laughing in a high-pitched, loud, and frenzied way.

Everything's going great. Right?

TWENTY-FIVE

Houston

I notice my parents exchange worried glances a handful of times as we drive across the country to Houston. Mathias rented a house for us in Houston's Rice Village neighborhood. When we pull up with the U-Haul, I'm relieved to see how beautiful it is. It even has a fenced-in grassy yard for the dogs. Before my parents fly back to Wisconsin, I talk with them about how Mathias has agreed to see his psychiatrist immediately to evaluate his medication levels. Mom and Dad breathe easier. I want to make this relationship work, and I'm willing to dive into the trenches with Mathias while he works to find the right dosage of mood stabilizers.

The problem is, Mathias doesn't make the appointment with the psychiatrist. He also rarely takes his medicine. Since moving in together, I remind him every day, and more often than not, he still won't take it. *Oh, wise Universe, what's going on?*

Mathias self-medicates with alcohol. He regularly drinks an entire 1.5-liter bottle of wine—the equivalent of about ten glasses—by himself in one sitting, followed by a couple of beers. Then he passes out. The sugary sour stench from his liver working in overdrive seeps out of his pores and through his chronic belches for days after each binge. Yet he denies he has a drinking problem and is irritable if I try to talk about it.

Soon after we arrive in Texas, his parents visit us, and the next round of red flags appears.

At one point, his mother says, "Since you now live with Mathias, I'm no longer going to make him check in with me every day. I'm relieved someone is looking out for him."

Hold up now, say what? Oh no, siree, I did not sign up to be a mother to my new boyfriend.

After dinner, his father pulls me aside. "We know our son has a lot of issues, and we're very grateful you're here to take care of him." He places both hands on my shoulders and looks into my eyes. "I hope Mathias doesn't ruin your life."

Geez. What?

DEFCON 3. Heightened alert level.

As my trepidation with Mathias's unstable mental state grows, his father's warning echoes. Most days, Mathias has escalating angry outbursts over the most menial of things. Yet he continues to surprise me with deep insights about life and romantic gestures that leave me questioning whether my mounting unhappiness is unrelated to my new relationship. Am I having culture shock from adjusting to living in Texas?

One day, Mathias comes home from work and says, "The urban sprawl of Houston is stifling you, so we're going to Austin this weekend. I know you need access to nature to thrive, and you keep saying Houston is too much city for you."

He's right, it is. We drive to Austin and spend a packed weekend swimming in spring-fed pools, kayaking, and hiking. For the first time since moving to Texas, I'm carefree and happy. People in Austin are welcoming, there is live music everywhere, and it's a foodie town where we eat breakfast tacos in the morning, vegan salads for lunch, and juicy oak-smoked brisket from an eclectic food truck park for dinner.

On the drive back to Houston, feeling optimistic and safe with Mathias, I gush, "I want us to live in Austin, not Houston."

He smiles as he squeezes my hand and says, "One day we will."

My renewed enthusiasm for Mathias and our future together is short-lived. His mood swings grow more extreme and angrier. Within a month of moving in, I am walking on eggshells, afraid of rocking the boat in any way that might trigger an outburst.

He's upset that I don't want to get engaged right away. I explain that the purpose of my moving to Houston is so we can get to know one another better and explore our relationship, since we don't know each other well, which leads to many heated discussions. He angrily accuses me of having one foot in and one foot out of the relationship. He's terrified that I'll move out, which makes him even more possessive.

Mathias's pattern of drinking, unpredictable mood swings, and explosive temper, followed by apologetic loving words and gifts, continues for the first two months I live in Houston. During the third month, a paralyzing fear grips me. It starts with the prickling of the hairs on the back of my neck, followed by a burning sensation in my stomach that rockets up my torso, and then clamps my throat like a vise. When Mathias gets angry, the features of his face morph into someone or something virtually unrecognizable. I'm taking the blame and apologizing for things to defuse his anger. I'm terrified of him hurting me, or worse yet, Yoda.

I thought I had successfully put Harry in the past, and now I can't stop thinking about him. Even when we had problems, Harry never considered me a possession to be owned and controlled. He never lashed out. He was still tender and kind even when our relationship was on its last legs. Most importantly, I was never in danger living with him. I trusted him not to hurt me.

While Mathias has his wild mood swings, I'm riding my own emotional rollercoaster—oscillating between the highs of finally leaving Los Angeles and breaking free from Harry, and the lows of realizing that I can't help Mathias or save our relationship. After years of feeling that LA infused my life with negative, dark energy, it's a bitter irony to realize LA was far safer than my current situation in Houston.

My lowest point comes when Mathias finds me sitting on the bathroom floor, quietly crying while attempting to reassemble a pole shower caddy that came crashing down when I was cleaning the tub. My meltdown is not in proportion to the perceived crisis of my spilled shampoo on the tile floor. Of course, it isn't about the shampoo. In my quest to be strong, things built up to the point where I exploded over something small and became a sniveling mess of tears.

The Mathias whom I first fell into "deep like" with—one couldn't call it love yet—sits on the floor beside me, looks into my eyes, and compassionately soothes, "I'm worried about you."

I look into his eyes, wondering if something's wrong with me, wanting to trust his concern.

Gently taking me in his arms, Mathias says, "I love you. Everything will be okay. Maybe things aren't as bad as you think, and you are catastrophizing." He helps me up and leaves the bathroom to fix dinner.

I sniffle while thinking, *I love this wonderful man.* The tears instantly stop, and for the first time in my life, I experience a taste of the cycle of abuse. No wonder women have such a hard time leaving abusive relationships. On the one hand, they live in fear, and on the other hand, they live for the times when their abusive partners are loving and affectionate.

DEFCON 2. Armed forces ready to deploy and engage.

The next morning, Mathias and I are in our robes, sitting on the sofa, and drinking coffee. Yoda wanders up to Mathias with his tail wagging and nudges his hand with his nose, the hand holding his coffee mug, jostling it—a splash of coffee spills over.

With uncontrolled fury, Mathias smacks Yoda hard on the back and bellows, "GOD DAMN IT, YODA."

The mother bear awakens, and I stand up and yell, "Don't EVER hit my dog again!" Then, in a calmer, quieter voice, "If you ever hurt Yoda again, I will leave."

My words strike a nerve. Mathias's fear is that I will leave him. He knows he can't control me. He explodes. His rage is unlike any I've ever seen. His face goes red, his nostrils flare, and the veins pop out in his neck. Spitting, he yells, "Get out of the house! Move out!" his face inches from mine. With his hand clenched in a fist, his arm is shaking and raised partway. "You are a quitter. I hate you!" he roars. Then he runs to my closet. "I never want to see you again," he growls, hurling my clothes into the middle of the room.

I stand silently shaking in shock, with Yoda and Oliver hiding behind me. Mathias throws off his robe, quickly dresses, and slams the door. I hear the screech of his car's tires as he drives away. He doesn't answer my calls or text messages, which I send him that evening when he doesn't come home from work. At midnight, I know I need to sleep, but I fear what Mathias will do when he finally comes home. Will he be drunk? Will he be violent? Will he come home at all? So, I do something I never dreamed I would do in my own home. I lock Yoda and Oliver in the bedroom with me and block the door with my heavy cedar chest and a chair. I keep my phone and a heavy Maglite next to me in case I need to call 911 or need a weapon to defend myself. In that moment, three months after I moved my life across the country to Houston, I make another decision.

DEFCON 1. Maximum readiness. Immediate response. *I'm out of here.*

Mathias finally comes home at 2 a.m. He stumbles around and heads straight to the guest bedroom. In a post-binge-drinking stupor the next morning, he apologizes for his behavior and gushes about how much he loves me. He asks me to be patient and explains that we have experienced a "normal" growing pain in a new relationship.

Listening, I'm quiet and emotionless. There's nothing normal about Mathias coming unhinged the way he did.

He leaves for work, and then I get busy.

My parents aren't surprised when I call to say I need to move out. On the one hand, admitting to being such a bad judge of character is humbling; on the other hand, confiding in them is a relief.

I want to handle this breakup gently, discussing it with Mathias beforehand through a healthy, respectful dialogue. However, in conversation with my parents and with my knowledge of advice for women leaving abusive or potentially violent relationships, I know there will be no chance to have a candid talk with Mathias. I need to move out on the day that I tell him, and I need my dad and Chuck to be there in case anything goes wrong.

Knowing Houston will never be a city my heart will call home, Dad asks if I want to put my belongings in storage while I find a new apartment in LA.

After hesitating momentarily, I declare, "I'm not moving back. I'm moving to Austin."

My words surprise me as much as they surprise Dad. I've only been to Austin once, when Mathias took me there for the weekend. I don't know anyone there, I don't know the city at all, and I don't have work there. Plus, Harry is in LA. (Wait, am I not ready to admit things are over with Harry after all?) Yet I can feel it: The energy of Austin calls to me in a way like none I've ever experienced anywhere in the world. Austin is the only city in Texas that has given me a home vibe. An affordable, outdoorsy paradise, it combines urban sophistication with a tree-hugging, artistic, open-minded sensibility. Austinites seem to embrace their authentic selves and celebrate expressions of individuality. Since the first day of my road trip, I've believed the road would lead me to my answer. I'm beginning to trust it has done so. Austin could be the place where I will finally find shama. I need to live there.

Upon hearing my seemingly random decision, my parents encourage me and are even excited for me. They don't judge; they support me—just as they did ten months ago when I started seeking change in my life through the U.S. highways.

The following two weeks are a blur of stealth phone calls and covert emails. Chuck finds a mover who promises to pack up everything and move me out in four hours. Dad and Chuck book flights to Houston. On Craigslist, I find an Austin real estate agent named Angele who emails rental property listings to a secret email account I set up. I only confide in my family and a couple of close friends to avoid the risk of Mathias finding out my plans and becoming unhinged again. Perhaps on some level, he already knows, because he's angry and hostile during the entire last two weeks I am here, leaving me emotionally exhausted.

Then, the eve before move-out day, right after Dad texts to say he's settled in a hotel a couple of blocks away and that Chuck's flight from LA just landed, Mathias comes home from work with a bouquet of flowers.

In a soulful and deliberate tone, he says, "Kee Kee, I have no excuse for my recent behavior. Since I've only taken my medication a few days this month, I'm worried I've been sabotaging our relationship. When I spoke with my parents earlier today, they reminded me that you are one of the best things to come into my life in a long time. It's true! Kee Kee, if I blow it with you, my family will never speak to me again."

While he jests, I can feel his remorse and concern that he's gone too far in his recent behavior. This Mathias, warm, genuine, gentle, humble, and honest, is the one with whom I had wanted to build a future. Yet, as Starr predicted, Mathias's demons run deep, and unfortunately, the good Mathias has been making fewer and fewer appearances since I moved to Houston.

Early the next morning, the sun makes a stripe-like shadow pattern on the white duvet as it shines through the horizontal slats of the Venetian blinds. My adrenaline is already surging. Mathias stayed up late painting and drinking and passed out on the sofa, so I'm alone in bed with the dogs. Oliver is snoring—it's remarkable that such a loud noise can come out of such a tiny body. *Sweet Oliver, I am going to miss you.* So is Yoda, as the two dogs have become inseparable. I picked this day to move because Mathias finally scheduled an appointment with his psychiatrist at 9 a.m. My idea is to tell him right before he leaves the house, hoping that he still goes, and the psychiatrist will be there for him.

At 8 a.m. sharp, Dad and Chuck pull up outside the house in their rented silver SUV. I text them that I'm about to tell Mathias, and the plan is that they'll come in the unlocked front door if I don't text again in ten minutes to let them know I'm okay. Microscopic beads of sweat break out in the tiny groove of flesh above my upper lip. It's do-or-die time.

"Mathias, can we talk?"

He sits in the armchair across from the sofa where I'm sitting and gives me a confused, concerned look while he finishes buttoning up his dress shirt.

"I'm so sorry, but this relationship isn't working for me, and I agree with you. It's better if I move out." My voice is quivering. "I still care about you, but we moved forward too fast. We're mismatched pieces of cloth."

I want to throw in something about his alcoholism and need for medication to stabilize his bipolar disorder, but I don't. We've had that conversation before, and the best way to keep him calm is to speak in a way that doesn't place blame. I clasp my hands together to keep them from shaking.

He is quiet. Finally, he whispers one word. "When?"

"The movers are coming today."

His jaw goes slack, and his eyebrows knit together.

As I explain, he stands up and slowly walks away while my voice trails off. He doesn't ask questions or want to hear my words. He goes into the backyard and makes a phone call, likely to his mother. He sits on a deck chair, his forehead in his left hand while he talks. Instead of being angry as I had feared, he looks distraught. My heart is breaking. I have never hurt another human being as deeply as I've wounded Mathias.

Without any words to me, Mathias leaves. I call Dad and tell him they can come inside, and I throw myself into Dad's arms first and then into Chuck's. They assure me that I couldn't have left any other way and that it could be the wake-up call Mathias needs to take his medication, get a grip on his anger, and stop drinking. Or not. It crushes me that Mathias didn't want to talk, hear my reasons, or listen to my apologies. I had barely sputtered, "I'm moving," when he shut me out. I know

I've made the right decision. For once, I have no shred of self-doubt—I am leaving to protect myself and Yoda from Mathias's abuse. So why do I feel as though I'm the crummiest human being on the planet? The only thing that keeps me from curling up into the fetal position and hiding from the world is that the movers arrive. To avoid trauma for the dogs from the chaos, I take Yoda and Oliver to doggie daycare. The following hours are a blur of boxes and packing tape. Then it is done.

I call Mathias. "Oliver is home from doggie daycare, and we're leaving."

"Okay."

"I'm sorry—"

He hangs up.

After this final exchange with Mathias, he doesn't return emails or calls over the next couple of weeks. I finally recognize that the kindest thing to do is to let him hate me, be furious, and feel betrayed. The combination of guilt for hurting him and relief for being free of a relationship with a man who is a ticking time bomb overrides my need for Mathias to like me.

The moving company is storing my belongings until I find a place to rent. The next day, after returning the rental car and dropping Chuck off at the airport, Dad, Yoda, and I drive to Austin and look at rental units that Angele has lined up for us to see. I fall in love with a little bright blue house with a yard abundant with southern live oak trees. Angele tells us that deer regularly wander through the neighborhood. It has a woodsy feel with a view of the state capitol from the end of the driveway.

The lease doesn't start until August, so Dad and I spend the next three days driving Princess with Yoda back to Wisconsin. Enjoying the last couple of weeks of July with my family at my parents' lake house will be restorative, giving me time to process the whirlwind of the past few months. This second road trip with my dad reminds me of the first one, over fifteen years ago, when he helped me move to Los Angeles. Like the first time around, this cross-country drive is a special experience. Dad listens to my regrets and fears as I lamely express them through choked emotion. We have evening cocktails in our hotel room each night. We spend hours upon hours in the car together, sometimes in silence, lost in thought, and other times jabbering on about things that only a father and daughter can deem important.

I try to put on a brave face for Dad about the decision to move to Austin, but my trust in my decision-making ability has been bruised by what happened with Mathias. I silently pray for a sign from the Universe that will prove that moving to Austin is a good thing. While Dad is driving, I take out my iPhone and search for the name of the street where my new rented cottage is: Rabb Road. The definitions I find for Rabb are "God," "One who looks over others with Divine love," and "the Universe." The real estate agent who showed us my new little blue house is named Angele, the Latin spelling of Angel, aka a divine messenger, or a messenger of God.

An inward smile spreads like a potent elixir of optimism. Those are my signs, loud and clear. All the many roads I've traveled over the past year have led me to Rabb Road, a road that, by its name, graces my life with a divine message that I'm still on the seeker's path, and moving to Austin is my next step in finding my peace, my shama.

TWENTY-SIX
Austin

"How long before we get to your house?" I climb back into the passenger seat at the gas station where we stopped to use the restroom.

Dad starts the car. "We're only about three hundred miles out. A glass of Early Times on the rocks is calling my name."

Thinking about the glass of Sauvignon Blanc with my name written all over it, I glance at the gas gauge, which is less than half full. After what happened in Death Valley, I hesitate—should I point out the gas is getting low, and then mention my rule never to have less than a half tank of gas?

But I'm with Dad, and he's driving. We have enough gas to make it home; he'll make sure of it. I don't want to take the time to fill up because I'm tired, I want to hug Mom, and I want wine.

Of course, we don't make it there. We run out of gas on the shoulder of the interstate about ninety miles from my parents' house. After waiting for a tow truck for over an hour with I-95 traffic zooming by—now it's dark—a flatbed tow truck driver delivers us to a gas station a mile away with Dad in the truck's cab, and Yoda and me high up in Princess Leia the Prius, scared out of our minds.

While staying with my family, one night, we're sitting around the fire pit. Yoda's lead is tied to the leg of a table next to me with the thirty-foot cable I used on my road trip. With his supersonic dog hearing, he picks up something and takes off running into the darkness. The cable wraps around my ankle before I can stop him. It cuts deeply into the skin, leaving a two-inch bloody gash around the back side of my left ankle. It burns, causing me to limp when I walk. Thankfully, it isn't my driving ankle; I can drive back to Austin.

All these months of waiting to see if Starr's New Year's Day wax reading would come true. She predicted I would have car trouble and injure my ankle in July, and that's exactly what happened—another reminder of the wild gift of having Starr in my life.

Yoda and I take three days to drive to Texas, timing it so that we spend one night in an Austin hotel and arrive at our little blue house on the same morning as the moving truck. I've spent the past couple of days unpacking. The last box sits before me. Gently removing the bubble wrap, I lift out a carved stone Buddha head, relieved that it has remained intact. It's a prop from *Feast of Love*, one of the movies I worked on. The Buddha head was the base of a lamp in the house of the character played by Morgan Freeman. When we wrapped production, one of the producers gave it to me.

I place the statue on an end table next to the sofa and smile at my companion. "Old life meets new, Yoda. Here is our daily reminder to seek shama."

Yoda rolls over onto his back and wriggles joyfully, asking for a belly rub.

"Let's celebrate and go for a drive."

We end up at nearby Barton Creek, walking along the spring-fed tributary that flows from Barton Springs Pool into Lady Bird Lake, part of the Colorado River that runs through downtown Austin. While we sit on the creek bank, two swans gracefully paddle by in the crystal-clear, aquamarine waters, their dynamic webbed feet leaving sparkling rivulets in their wake. My mind drifts to all the people who have impacted my life, especially over the past year, and how each encounter on the path has somehow led me to live in Austin.

I've long been confused by the saying that people come into one's life for a reason, a season, or a lifetime. It makes more sense to say that no matter what, every single person comes into one's life for a reason. Yet some people hang around for a season and others for a lifetime.

Sometimes, people roll into my life with a cyclone of emotion and then leave with a bang before I can even begin to process what happened. At other times, the reason is clear, such as when someone helps me make a decision or forever changes how I look at a situation.

Some people are a blip on the radar, even though their actions or words stay with me for years.

That was the case when I was driving through Oklahoma on the way back to Austin from Wisconsin—a muscle spasm started in my mid-back that was so bad that I needed to stop immediately to stretch, and the only thing around was a fruit stand, so I pulled in. A frail, elderly man sat in an aluminum webbed lawn chair, quietly hunched over, looking at his wrinkled hands folded in his lap. A calico cat was on the ground next to him, and some burning trash was smoldering in the nearby field behind him. He stood up and shuffled over as I picked out some fruit. The cat followed him and stood by his side. I bought a box of peaches, and he introduced himself as Leland.

"Do you mind if I walk my dog in the field?"

"That's fine," Leland responded.

I grabbed Yoda's leash and let him out of the car. The cat started hissing, arched her back, and walked wide circles around Leland, her eyes never leaving Yoda during our walk.

After I put Yoda back in Princess, and before I carefully climbed in—with my back stretched—to drive away, I said to the man, "You have yourself a guard cat."

"This cat saved my life two nights ago."

It turns out that the smoldering trash was the smoking remains of his cottage.

"This here is a stray cat that sometimes hangs around here. I was asleep, and this cat here jumped through the window and landed on my chest. I woke up to find the roof on fire."

"Thank goodness you got out," I exclaimed. "Were you able to save anything?"

"Nope. The house and all my belongings burned to the ground. The cat hasn't left my side since."

"Do you have a place to stay now?"

He pointed to a one-room trailer with a yellow toilet on the ground outside facing the rural highway.

"My landlord owns the fruit stand, and he brought me this trailer to stay in. He said if I sell enough fruit, then he'll rebuild the cottage for me to live in."

I picked up a watermelon and handed him a twenty-dollar bill. Then, with a ball of emotion knotted in my throat, I told him how sorry I was for his loss.

"I'm an old man and I've been through a lot in my eighty-five years." He observed me with a toothless, crooked smile. "What I've learned is that bad stuff happens, and then it gits better."

Leland was unfazed by losing his house and his belongings. He was at peace with himself and his life. Looking at him, I wondered if the secret to finding shama is being eighty-five, owning nothing, and sitting on the side of the road selling fruit in Oklahoma.

Another time, over eight years ago, I parallel parked in Venice Beach, and when I got out of my car, a woman in a white SUV was shrieking at me out her window for taking her spot. I hadn't seen her waiting, so I apologized profusely. When I started to get into my car to give her the spot, she hurled obscenities while flipping me the bird and screeched off, leaving black skid marks on the road. Thinking about this incident still makes me cringe. I have no idea what I did wrong. Why did that happen? What was the lesson?

A lesson. That's it, the reason every single person comes into one's life. It may take years to figure out what that lesson is, but it's always there. Often, the more painful the experience, the more valuable it is for personal growth. So, whether my interaction with someone is happy, loving, hateful, or confusing, it's important to carry gratitude for that person making an appearance in my life. Sometimes, it's challenging. Occasionally, it's near impossible; I do my best.

There's a practice I keep in mind in my quest for shama: seeing the Divine in everyone. Some people call it God, others call it Source, the Universe, or the cosmic spark. Whatever it is, it's in all of us: in family, coworkers, every stranger on the street, and every politician, whether I like them or loathe them. Since the Divine is in everyone, we're all connected, and I can't live with shama unless I seek out that sacred miracle of existence. In everyone. While it's often challenging when I think of all the horrible, ugly things people do to one another, recognizing that common thread running through all of us is a step toward living with inner peace.

Wouldn't the world be more beautiful if we were grateful for the lessons people bring into our lives? If we took time to find *the reason* behind each person we encounter, there would be much less hostility, anger, and resentment, and more peace, love, and joy.

Maybe the cussing, angry, middle-finger-flipping SUV woman came into my life to teach me to be more aware of my surroundings. Leland appeared in my life to teach me optimism, to roll with the punches, and that "Bad stuff happens, and then it gits better."

A more recent lesson involves Mathias. We broke up, and it was messy. I guess that's an understatement. Already I can see the reason he came into my life. Because of him, I took a wild leap of faith and moved 1,600 miles across the country. For the first time, I took a chance on love without first overanalyzing it or asking others for their opinion. I didn't follow the rules; I followed an adventure. I may have subconsciously plunged so quickly into the relationship because I no longer wanted to call LA home. Yet I had big hopes for lasting love with Mathias. Although ours was not a forever relationship, I don't regret spontaneously moving to Houston to explore it. My experience with Mathias taught me that I'm a strong woman, strong enough to leave a relationship before it became dangerous. Strong enough to hurt someone I once cared about, to keep my dog and myself safe.

The two swans run and take flight, their majestic wings lifting them out of the water with a soft rhythmic humming as they fly downstream. I stretch my legs in front of me on the creek bank, and Yoda circles to reposition himself next to me, then plops his head on my thigh.

I close my eyes and say a silent prayer of gratitude to my sweet Yoda, my family, Beth, Starr, Art, Wyatt the cowboy, the angry woman in the SUV, Leland, all people who have touched my life in one way or another, the city of Los Angeles, and even Mathias. I thank them all. I will forever carry with me the lessons they've sent my way.

Eyes still closed in prayer, I feel a ripple of gratitude surge for Harry. We met at a formative time in my life after I'd moved across the country by myself for my dream job. I was in the process of making my first footprints in the sand of my adult life. Insecurities stemming from Harry's commitment phobia drove me to try different hats to become the woman I thought Harry wanted me to be—not a good dynamic. The silver lining was that, while trying to prove myself to Harry and win his love—through world travel, solo museum excursions, joining an improv troupe, reading books I never would have picked up, and reluctantly trying sushi for the first time—I figured out my interests, what makes me laugh, and what makes me cry, and yes, I learned that I freakin' love sushi. Thank you, Harry.

Now I can finally see *the reason* Harry came into my life was to push me to discover how large my life can be and the many scenic landscapes to explore within myself. This road trip has had reminders of Harry at virtually every bend in the road. But I've been holding on to the memory of our six years together too tightly. Since we broke up, I've subconsciously compared every man in my life to Harry, never giving anyone a realistic chance to measure up, and never giving myself permission to fully commit my heart to someone other than my first love. My post-Harry lovers have been competing with something fabricated in my mind. Dang, I was blind as a bat, until bang, one day it all fell into place.

My recollection of our relationship has been like a patchwork quilt, assembled solely of remnants of memories sewn together with threads of the past. But the quilt I've been carrying around only has the "good" pieces; I've left out the ragged ones. Those rough patches, so to speak, are the fabric scraps tucked away into the dark corners of my sewing kit. Much like creating a real quilt, in the end, my Harry-relationship quilt, made up of fragments of good memories, was much more beautiful than each piece standing on its own. It took this road trip to finally realize that this quilt is not illustrative of the actual relationship I had with Harry; rather, it reflects what I had hoped our relationship would one day be. It's time to unravel the threads and mothball that quilt.

My eyes flicker open. Across the creek from us, two men dressed in black pants and long-sleeved black shirts walk straight into the water. About twenty people gathered on the far bank begin singing and swaying back and forth. Then one man cups the back of the other man's head and immerses his entire body in the water. I'm witnessing a baptism, a spiritual rebirth of this man. What perfect symbolism. The past year has been a time of spiritual rebirth for me. It's the year I buried Goody Two-Shoes by welcoming change, breaking out of the mold, and living life my way. This year, I moved to Texas and became a cowgirl. So to speak.

We climb into Princess and start the short drive home. Yoda is looking out the window with his ears pricked forward as he takes in our new neighborhood. I smile at him in the rearview mirror, then return my eyes to the road. At some point over the past year, the conviction that I've been sleepwalking through life replaced the frequent fears and tears.

The touchstones I once leaned on to find my way have served their time, and now I'm ready to let them fall away. I'm awakening to a life that is true to myself. Look at the adventure of this road trip. The freshest, most enlightening moments happened when my guard was down, with no expectations or plans. Leaving the safety zone and letting go of the rigid constraints and rule-following with which I have always tried to control my destiny opened the room for things to happen naturally.

I've learned that the Universe is on my side, and it would never allow me to make a change without giving me what I need to make that change successfully. It constantly gives me signs, signs to help me understand and signs to help me find my way. Now I always watch for those magical moments—signals to do the unusual, unimaginable, and the unexplainable.

I put my decade-old "I Welcome Change" sticky note to the test this past year: I welcomed change. I didn't know what would happen. By not resisting, change arrived.

Cowboy Wyatt in San Antonio delivered an enduring metaphor for bringing shama into life—the cowgirl vibe is one of freedom. Making my way, kicking up my spurs, and saddling my horse. I fooled myself into thinking there's something comfortable and secure with living a life like everyone else's. The new cowgirl in me wants to straddle my horse with the reins loose and free, and lasso a bona fide life of being true to myself, challenging myself daily, and honoring those distinctive quirks undeniably unique to me. That's the spirit. The cowgirl spirit. Without the cows. Or horses.

As I turn Princess onto Rabb Road, I reflect on how, when I stopped chasing shama all over the country by running away from my life for ten months, I sat still long enough to realize I find shama by being present in my life. As it turns out, I didn't need to go anywhere. Shama is always inside me.

Of all the lessons of the road, my most priceless is that my journey to inner peace never ends. It isn't supposed to. Inner peace is fleeting. It comes and goes. Life is often complicated, messy, and heart-wrenching. Part of the human experience is learning to sort through the chaos of life and find moments of peace in the darkest places. To do that, I start within.

I pull into the driveway and park. I gaze up at the little blue house. Our new home on Rabb Road will be a magical place for new faces and longtime friendships, rain or shine, and more learning. I wonder how long I'll stay here. What is possible now that I know shama is always here, wherever I am?

I reach over my shoulder to rub the side of Yoda's neck. He's standing on the back seat, waiting eagerly to see why we stopped.

"Yoda, we're home."

EPILOGUE

Yoda and I were together for twelve and a half years—a quarter of my life. After moving to Austin, we continued to take road trips a few times a year. Then love stepped in (for both of us).

My work combined filmmaking, consulting, and writing. One of my clients was a company developing a children's musical for Dubai. The company's CEO wanted us to work with Eric Troyer, a singer and keyboardist with an impressive resume as a background vocalist on many megahits from the 1980s. Now, he was in a classic rock band that he joined as Electric Light Orchestra Part II, currently touring as The Orchestra Starring ELO and ELO Part II Former Members. In a small world twist of fate, I'd been friends with Parthenon Huxley, the guitar player in this band, since the late 1990s. We went to the band's concert in the Denver area, and then Eric, the CEO, and I spent a week together in Vail, developing the musical.

Even with his phenomenal success in rock and roll, Eric remains one of the most humble, honest, warm, and kind souls I've ever met. As the months progressed, our relationship deepened into something far more intimate—friends becoming lovers. I felt something I had never experienced: a love that felt like *home*. Our bond grew stronger through mutual trust, respect, passion, laughter, and a profound acceptance of each other, scars and all.

Four years after Yoda and I moved to Austin, Eric helped us uproot again by loading up Princess Leia and moving us to his home in bucolic New Jersey woods to live with him. Yoda spent the last year and a half of his life transitioning from being a city dog to being a rural dog. The melodies of birds replaced the noise of traffic, and the only pedestrians around were a family of six deer who called our property home. We both quickly took to the gentle pace of country living and thrived by forming a family of three. Eric was very tender with Yoda when he couldn't manage the climb to the bedroom because of his arthritic hips, even carrying him up and down the steep, narrow steps.

Ultimately, when Yoda's age (between fourteen and a half and fifteen years old) caught up with him, it became clear that the many painkillers we gave him daily were no longer working. He lost interest in eating, and his legs could no longer reliably support him. Even with his body giving out, Yoda's lovable, loyal, and curious personality was with him until the end.

The final day of my furry shama warrior's life, February 28, 2017, began with baking a "Yoda Pie" in his honor. The three of us ate the apple pie for lunch, and Yoda devoured his piece (an impressive feat, given we had spent the last month begging him to eat). With our first bite, we said, "Thank you, Yoda," to express our gratitude for him enriching our lives.

Later that night, Eric and I said goodbye to Yoda, with a heartful celebration of his large life to set him free. After the vet sedated Yoda, my friend Dorry Bless, a Life-Cycle Celebrant, conducted a beautiful ceremony to commemorate his life. It involved sage, poetry, Tibetan bells, celebratory words about his magnificent adventures, prayer, and an original song by Eric that he wrote for Yoda, singing through tears as he played it on the grand piano.

Yoda had been near-deaf for the past couple of years, only hearing our whistles, but his favorite spot in the house was next to the grand piano when Eric was playing, feeling the vibrations. Even in his sedated state, I'm convinced Yoda could hear the music and feel love, comfort, and safety as Eric sang him his beautiful song.

Next, I read him a letter thanking him for our shared life. Soon thereafter, the vet set him free as we held him in our arms.

Yoda, my shama guru, delivered his final lesson to me that night: somehow, some way, I needed to find shama amidst the heartbreak of losing him. I had been preparing myself for a couple of years as I watched Yoda slow down and become more fragile with age, believing I had finally arrived at a place where I would celebrate his life more than I would mourn. I can now say with absolute certainty that there is no way one can prepare oneself for the loss of a beloved pet. But in the letter I read to him, I promised Yoda I would find shama amidst the grief after his death. A promise made on a deathbed is a promise one must keep. But how?

I started by zealously baking Yoda Pies. Whenever the tears overwhelmed me, I would walk into the kitchen and make a Yoda Pie. Rather than cry while mixing the dough, rolling it out, preparing the filling, decorating the top with hearts, peace symbols, and his name cut out of dough, and baking it, I would celebrate the amazing adventures Yoda had during his long life and how this wonderful dog helped me find shama by giving me the courage to live an authentic life.

I must have made close to one hundred Yoda Pies in the five months following his transition: fruit pies, savory pies, cream pies, meringues, custards, galettes—if a fruit or vegetable was in the house, odds were it would end up in a pie. We couldn't possibly eat that many pies, so I gave many away and froze others.

Despite my deep grief, I was putting into play the lesson I learned on the road while visiting Beth at the American Gothic House. She was right; pie heals, pie is comfort food, and pie does make people happy. Seeing the smiles the Yoda Pies brought to people's faces was evidence that Yoda's legacy would live on.

Although baking Yoda Pies helped me deal with grief surges, I still needed to figure out how to find inner peace while my heart was hurting more than I ever knew possible.

I traveled with Eric's band for the first six weeks after we lost Yoda, because I couldn't bear to be in the house alone, and in an attempt to outrun my sadness. It didn't work and instead forced me to face my pain head-on. I drowned in my tears as I stared into the turquoise waters of the Caribbean Sea, crying so much that there were light scabs on the tender skin under my eyes; I choked back sobs while wandering around Disney World, the self-proclaimed "Happiest Place on Earth"; and, in the Holy City of Jerusalem, I prayed for Yoda's transition in the Church of the Holy Sepulchre. It really was just like Yoda to time his passing for me to go with the band to Israel, where people greet one another with "shalom," a word that means peace/shama.

After touring with the band, I continued to travel to scatter Yoda's ashes in all the special places we had lived together: in our New Jersey yard in the roots of a Rising Sun Redbud tree; in Austin in the backyard of the little blue house we shared; in Wisconsin, off the bow of my parents' pontoon boat (his favorite place in the world); and at the beach in Santa Monica, where our life together began.

The six months following Yoda's passing were the most heart-crushing of my life. Simultaneously, they were also some of the most important. That's because I didn't deny myself a time of mourning, and instead surrendered to the pain. Two constants in life are love and loss; heartache from the loss of love is a natural part of the human experience. Yoda, my greatest teacher, wanted me to learn from his death. So, I dove deep into grief to discover why God gives us loss.

Here's what I learned:

In our culture, we're not encouraged to honor grief, especially mourning the loss of pets. We shove the sadness down, hiding it inside, making us numb. But by surrendering to grief, something beautiful happens: the veil separating us from the invisible partially lifts. Grief brings a stillness in the moment and, when we let it, a profound connection with nature. Colors are brighter, and the textures of the world are more vivid. At times, I was able to *feel* nature and its healing energy. During this period of bottomless sorrow, I also experienced a different, yet still mighty connection with Yoda through some of the most mystical experiences of my life.

Once I emerged from deep mourning and life began to return to normal (although normal changed because my identity was no longer "Kee Kee and Yoda"), the veil lowered, and with it, some of that brilliant, rich, ethereal sparkle of the world lessened. My intense connection with Yoda slipped away. Strangely, I was *sad* that I was no longer intensely grieving.

Loss is an inescapable part of life, and I must deal with more of it as I get older. Perhaps through the cavernous sorrow of losing loved ones, both human and animal, the Universe is preparing me for my inevitable death. Loss is also a reminder always to be grateful for the small miracles of each day while I have them: the sweet burst of a tomato eaten right off the vine, the iridescent shimmer of a rainbow after a storm; the gentle touch of my lover's hand as he walks past; and, of course, the wag of a tail and a nuzzle from a cold, wet snout.

A year after Yoda's passing, our friend Janice, the mayor of Clinton, NJ, wedded Eric and me in a private ceremony on the banks of a meandering, gentle river in front of a historic 19th-century grist mill next to a picturesque cascading waterfall. A couple of months later, we traveled to Wisconsin and renewed our vows in front of my family, with Beth officiating the ceremony. She baked us a Yoda Pie so that Yoda would be a part of our union. The pie sat in a wicker basket on a table next to us when we exchanged our vows. When I said, "I do," I glanced at the Yoda Pie and blinked hard.

My sweet Yoda taught me the meaning of unconditional love. I may never have made it to this altar with Eric without our fateful *Seeking Shama* road trip. Yoda quietly cracked open my heart, gave me the courage to welcome change, and stood by my side as I confronted and healed my pain. Our journey together taught me to accept and love myself without apology and to embrace the importance of grounding myself in my self-worth. Yoda led me to a place in life where I was finally ready to give and receive love fully, and to begin a fresh chapter with my husband by my side.

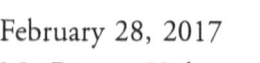

February 28, 2017
My Dearest Yoda,

It has been the greatest honor of my life to be your human. I'm filled with gratitude that you chose me twelve and a half years ago. We have been family from the moment you first looked at me with those big, caramel-colored eyes, and I felt you looking straight into my soul. We were a team of two for most of the time, and finally we have become a team of three (oh, how happy I am to have finally given you a daddy!).

You have been the greatest teacher of my life. But of course, that's the case, given you share a name with the wisest and most masterful of all Jedi Masters. It *had* to be you, Yoda. It couldn't have been any other dog to show me the Force. You are a shama warrior.

I was pretty sad and lost when we met. You saved me. Then you led me on the most transforming journey of my life as we drove for five months seeking shama. Here's the wonderful thing: I actually found it through our epic road trip! Of course, afterward, I realized that inner peace is fleeting. It comes and goes. Life is complicated, messy, and heart-wrenching. But I think it's supposed to be. I think that those of us who embody the human form are put here to learn to find shama in every moment of the chaos of life.

Oh, the life we have shared! We've lived at the beach, in the hills, on a lake, and in the woods. California, Texas, Wisconsin, and now New Jersey have been home to us. And of course, Princess Leia the Prius was also our home as we drove around the country together. You've visited more states than many people. What a big, bold, beautiful life we've built together.

You have made sure that I safely arrived at the place in life you were supposed to deliver me to. You have prepared me to continue putting all the lessons we learned on the road into practice. I am eternally grateful to you, Master Yoda. Finding shama in each situation that is presented to me will be a constant practice for the rest of my life. I'm ready now to do that without you. I'll be okay, I promise. I will not pull on your energies when you are gone, but I will absolutely love you in a new, magnificent way.

I'm going to miss you. And right now, I can't imagine life without you in it. But that's the wonderful thing about life, right? We can't imagine what beauteous thing might be just around the corner.

You have touched so many people throughout your life. You are so loved, even by people who have never met you. But no one has ever loved you the way that I love you. What a gift it has been to share a life with you. Our bond has been such that at times I've felt we are one. But the time has come to untangle our souls and go our separate ways.

I'm going to miss your bouncy bat ears, your itsy-bitsy mohawk, your fur that is still as silky soft as a bunny, your soulful eyes, and our walks together. I'm going to miss the way you bury your head into my chest, almost like you can't get close enough. I will miss *just being* together as you lie under my desk at my feet.

My sweet prince, it's time for you to transition to formlessness and move on to a glorious place where you no longer are in pain. You can let go of the heavy load of worry that you have carried in this lifetime. Your separation anxiety has been filled with worry about protecting me. But I no longer need you to protect me. I'm safe. I promise.

Thank you for choosing me as your human. Thank you for teaching me patience and unconditional love. Thank you for being my protector and for giving me courage. And thank you for teaching me about inner peace. Now it is time for me to find shama amidst the grief when you are gone. I'll do it, honey; I promise.

I'm excited for you, my precious one. Oh, what wonderful freedom awaits you. Daisy, Leroy, Tessa, Molly, and Ollie are all waiting for you. Go to them. It's time for you to slip into eternal shama.

I love you with every ounce of my being.

—*Kee Kee*

ACKNOWLEDGMENTS

Mining for crystals involves separating the gangue—waste rock and unwanted materials—from the valuable gemstones. It's a necessary but often tedious process for a rock hound. There was a lot of gangue in my early drafts of this book, and I have so many people to thank for helping me treasure hunt. This book exists because of the following people, who are real gems in my life.

To my readers, thank you for helping me sort through the gravel to find precious stones worth keeping: Laura Archdeacon, Lynne Litt, Roy Rivers, Val Sivilli, Beata Swiderska, Kerrin Thompson, and my mom.

A special thank you to Angela Hynes and Dorry Bless for your encouragement and for delivering substantial and honest notes about my writing, even when it was uncomfortable to do so. You are true friends.

To Beth Howard, thank you for fielding crisis calls during my road trip and while I was writing this book. You championed me as an author and helped me believe in myself when I wanted to quit. Your invaluable editing helped shape this book, and your friendship continues to carry me.

To the many people who lifted me up and supported me in numerous ways during my road trip and during the writing of this book: John and Margaret Bohnel, Chuck Champion, Karen Cotter, Starr Fuentes, Kim Goldman, Holly Herndon, Art Jackson,

Rick Kurek, Todd Lieman, Jake Martin, Tracy Monaco, Alissa Murgia, David Robbins, Dawn Sinko (who took the photo on the cover of this book minutes before Yoda and I pulled out of the driveway and started on our epic journey), Shanti Sosienski, Ernest Thompson, Brad Warner, and Seth Witcher.

Thank you to the butter in my life, my family, including my seestars, Deb Miller, Didi Buckley, and Betsy Hemminger. Thank you to my parents, Jim and Nancy Buckley, for passing down the road trip gene and for always believing in me. I love you.

Huge thanks to my first editor, Jennifer Pooley, for helping me envision the format for this book. I extend so much gratitude to the team at Wellness Writers Press for their expertise and creativity in bringing *Seeking Shama* across the finish line: Julie Colvin, Leila Summers, Lynn Thompson, and Jane Spencer.

Having a dog with severe separation anxiety requires a strong support team. I owe a debt of gratitude to those friends who loved Yoda like their own and cared for him, allowing me to have a social life: Lisa Renaud and John Rosenthal, Gayle Shubin, Rover Kennels in Culver City, David Lee, Linda Wisniewski, and The Puppy Patch.

Thank you to the many people who opened their homes, fed me, and shared their stories when I was on the road seeking shama. While there are too many of you to list individually, I'm grateful to you all.

Thank you to Eric Troyer for your thoughtful notes on the many drafts of this manuscript, for the beautiful theme song for this book, and for forming Team Awesome with me. I love you forever and always.

Lastly, thank you, Yoda, for teaching me about inner peace. And thank you, Lunabelle, for teaching me that I can love another dog again.

ABOUT THE AUTHOR

Kee Kee Buckley is a New Jersey-based writer, filmmaker, speaker, and rock band manager who infuses her life's work with the sacred pursuit and quiet transformation of shama—inner peace. Bringing a deep reverence to the connection between mind, body, and spirit, Kee Kee is an activist dedicated to raising awareness about the dangers of antibiotic overuse and the vital role of the gut microbiome in the harmony of physical and mental well-being. She draws on the foundation of her decades of personal study, spiritual practice, and soul-centered speaking, and her advocacy has taken her from keynote stages to Capitol Hill and multiple FDA hearings. Kee Kee lives in the woods with her musician husband, Eric, their Malinois-mix rescue dog, Lunabelle, and a family of friendly deer. They all remind her daily of life's micro moments of magic.

keekeebuckley.com
Facebook.com/seekingshama
Instagram: @seekingshama